KAITLYN SCHIESS

FOREWORD BY MICHAEL WEAR

THE
Liturgy

SPIRITUAL
FORMATION
FOR THE
SAKE OF OUR
NEIGHBOR

OF
Politics

An imprint of InterVarsity
Downers Grove, Illinc

InterVarsity Press
P.O. Box 1400, Downers Grove, IL 60515-1426
ivpress.com
email@ivpress.com

InterVarsity Press® is the book-publishing division of InterVarsity Christian Fellowship/USA®, a movement of students and faculty active on campus at hundreds of universities, colleges, and schools of nursing in the United States of America, and a member movement of the International Fellowship of Evangelical Students. For information about local and regional activities, visit intervarsity.org.

While any stories in this book are true, some names and identifying information may have been changed to protect the privacy of individuals.

Cover design and image composite: Faceout Studio
Interior design: Jeanna Wiggins
Images: city street map: © Fourleaflover / iStock / Getty Images Plus
          badge illustration: © Francesco Zerilli/Zerillimedia/Science Photo Library

ISBN 978-0-8308-4830-0 (print)
ISBN 978-0-8308-5340-3 (digital)

Library of Congress Cataloging-in-Publication Data
Names: Schiess, Kaitlyn, author. | Wear, Michael R., 1988- author of foreword.
Title: The liturgy of politics : spiritual formation for the sake of our neighbor / Kaitlyn Schiess ; foreword by Michael Wear.
Description: Downers Grove, IL : IVP, [2020] | Includes bibliographical references.
Identifiers: LCCN 2020027318 (print) | LCCN 2020027319 (ebook) | ISBN 9780830848300 (paperback) | ISBN 9780830853403 (ebook)
Subjects: LCSH: Christianity and politics—United States. | Christians—Political activity—United States. | Spiritual formation—Political aspects—United States.
Classification: LCC BR526 .S286 2020 (print) | LCC BR526 (ebook) | DDC 261.70973—dc23
LC record available at https://lccn.loc.gov/2020027318
LC ebook record available at https://lccn.loc.gov/2020027319

P 25 24 23 22 21 20 19 18 17 16 15 14 13 12 11 10 9 8 7 6 5 4
Y 42 41 40 39 38 37 36 35 34 33 32 31 30 29 28 27 26 25 24 23 22

"What hath the upper room to do with the Oval Office? What does the Spirit have to do with the Senate? In *The Liturgy of Politics*, Kaitlyn Schiess offers an insightful framework for thinking about these two at-first-glance antagonists. Many evangelicals nowadays seem to be suffering from worldview dissonance—shunning political engagement altogether because it's 'dirty work' or shirking genuine and careful participation because dogmatism and bumper-sticker responses roll off the tongue more easily. Schiess offers a careful and sustained via media that emphasizes the movement, timing, and practices of the church, which instill a vision for gathering community and reforming political participation. With fluent brilliance, Schiess does this by looking to ancient and contemporary voices such as Augustine, Karl Barth, and Jamie Smith. She reminds us that every time we enter that dusty, smelly building with well-worn pews, we throw ourselves at the right way to move and live and have our being—in shared spaces with our neighbor in the world!"

Kyle David Bennett, associate professor of philosophy and chair of the theology and philosophy department at Caldwell University

"*The Liturgy of Politics* is a much-needed discourse on effective leadership in politics and caring for our culture. I have been following Kaitlyn's important voice for some time now, and I am delighted to have her contribution for our journey toward the New."

Makoto Fujimura, artist, author of *Culture Care* and *Silence and Beauty*

"Many young evangelicals—weary of politics and the culture wars—have begun to disengage from political life. Tired of the narrow-minded politics of the right and left, these evangelicals long for something more—something beyond ideology and sound bites. Kaitlyn Schiess has answered her generation's call. Drawing on Scripture, history, and contemporary political theology, she offers a robust and accessible political ethic that avoids the old pitfalls of the Christian right and left. She deftly explores how worship and spiritual disciplines can not only liberate evangelicals from destructive political ideologies but actively move them into God's alternative political mission of public justice and shalom."

Matthew Kaemingk, assistant professor of Christian ethics and associate dean, Fuller Theological Seminary

"This is the book I have been waiting for! There could hardly be a more important topic for our cultural moment than the connection between Christian formation and politics. Kaitlyn Schiess persuasively and powerfully argues that Christians are being deeply formed by the political currents in which we swim, although we don't often realize it. She then casts a beautiful biblical and theological vision for intentional Christian formation that, by God's grace, shapes us into disciples who love God as we attend to the life of the world. While giving detailed attention to how and why we practice prayer, Bible reading, worship, Sabbath, and the sacraments, Schiess casts a sweeping and winsome vision of the Christian life, including political engagement and so much more. This book will itself be deeply formative for all who read it. It needs to be read by pastors, youth ministers, worship leaders, small groups, college and seminary students, and all who care about faithful discipleship and formation today."

Kristen Deede Johnson, dean and professor of theology and Christian formation at Western Theological Seminary

"Neighborliness is a skill one must learn. We do not enter the world fully equipped to be faithful citizens or fruitful members of our local communities. Rather, we learn the skills, virtues, and habits that are required for faithful participation in common life over time. Or, too often, we don't learn any of those things, and we set out on the quest to live honorable lives in our homes, neighborhoods, cities, states, and nation radically unprepared for the challenges laid before us. Kaitlyn Schiess's *The Liturgy of Politics* is a worthy reflection on where mature community members come from and how our churches, schools, and neighborhoods can be shaping such people now. I am happy to commend this fine study to you."

Jake Meador, editor-in-chief of *Mere Orthodoxy* and author of *In Search of the Common Good: Christian Fidelity in a Fractured World*

TO MY PARENTS

Of every wonderful gift you've given me,

nothing else can compare to a childhood

spent watching two faithful Christians use

their gifts for the sake of the world.

AND TO KENDRA WOO

I want to be more like you when I grow up.

Contents

FOREWORD *by Michael Wear* 1

1 APOLITICAL OR UNEXAMINED 5
What Spiritual Formation Has to Do with Politics

2 THE LITURGY OF POLITICS 22
Loves and Loyalties

3 OF THIS WORLD 39
The Gospels of Prosperity, Patriotism, Security, and Supremacy

4 FOR THE LIFE OF THE WORLD 57
Spiritual Formation and Public Life

5 A STORY TO LIVE INTO 74
Scripture and Political Formation

6 *EKKLĒSIA* 93
The Church as a Training Ground for Political Engagement

7 THE RHYTHM OF OUR LIVES 114
Time, Music, Confession

8 BENT ON THE COMING KINGDOM OF GOD 135
Spiritual Disciplines and Political Formation

9 A CONFESSING CITY 155
Reading Politics with Augustine

10 CREATION REDEEMED 169
Eschatology and Political Formation

EPILOGUE: *Shalom* 188

ACKNOWLEDGMENTS 191

NOTES 193

Foreword

MICHAEL WEAR

Before you read this book, I want you to take a moment. Consider your expectations. Consider your posture. Our political imagination is so saturated with angry voices on talk radio and cable news, with podcasts narrowly tailored for their audience, and political campaigns that have the ability to speak to everyone and no one at all, that we often think this is all politics is and all that it ever could be. No one talks about politics, or gets involved in politics, to serve. Only the sentimental believe it to be otherwise. Politics is about winning—winning for the right reasons and the right causes is about the best we can imagine.

Before you read this book, imagine this: you are a member of a church that has decided that its life together is both influenced by and influencing politics. Just as importantly, your congregation has decided that it does not quite understand how and why this is happening or what to do about it. Given your church's recognition that politics is both vital and not understood, you have decided as a body to commission someone to dedicate a concentrated period of study and thought to the subject and report back.

This book is that report.

That is to say, I want you to receive this book not as a challenge but as a gift. This book will read to you like an act of service, and it is refreshingly free of the kind of manipulation that is so rampant in so much of the communication about politics today. I want you to approach it with a welcoming and open spirit. You can feel safe enough to do so.

Politics, of course, is not often safe. Though we can lose sight of it as politics serves as fodder for small talk and comedy sketches, politics deals with force and harm, with systems and structures, with benefits bestowed and benefits withheld, with matters of war and welfare. If politics constituted posturing and put-downs alone, if politics was merely a forum for self-expression that we could cleanly opt out of, then Christians would certainly have better uses for their time. But for Christians, politics is not important because we ascribe great value to political ideas, but because we ascribe great value to the human person. It is because we know that politics affects our neighbors, for good and for ill, which is why you are reading this book and Kaitlyn Schiess has written it.

The word *prophetic* is regularly misused in conversations about faith and politics. *Prophetic* is often a euphemism for "boldly and unapologetically calling for what I already support." It takes courage to speak into the political scene today, to ask people to be attentive to the character of our political life and the character of our lives as citizens. We think it is prophetic to condemn our political leaders, and we call for policies that stretch the boundaries of public opinion, but I believe the real prophetic call is the one issued in this book: the call to attend to the kind of people we are as we participate in politics. It is to consider spiritual formation for the sake of our neighbor.

Kaitlyn writes here as a voice for a new generation, though she reflects on old ideas and old sources—from Plato to the Old Testament prophets to Augustine. With great insight, she describes some of the modern forces that have led us to this moment in our politics, and helps us to understand why evangelical political involvement looks and feels the way it does today.

It is time that we become attentive to what politics is doing to us, what it tries to do to us, and what we, wittingly or not, are doing to our politics. The formative power of politics has been a major concern of my work and life. As someone who served in the White House and worked in presidential politics, I saw the power politics can have over people and the way that the desires and affections of citizens influence how government works. I described some of this in my first book, *Reclaiming Hope,* in which I argued that "the state of our politics is a reflection of the state of our souls." Since that book was released in 2017, I have spent a lot of time thinking about what naturally follows from that statement: our politics cannot improve in a lasting way unless its incentive structure changes, and the incentive structure that guides our politics will not fundamentally change unless we become a different kind of people.

Spiritual formation is not as enigmatic as we sometimes make it out to be. When we put our faith in Jesus, we put our whole selves under his care. Our willingness to identify with certain theological ideas is one thing, but the extent to which our life and behavior reflects actual confidence and belief in truths about God and his kingdom is another. What was most remarkable about Jesus was not just that he said things such as "love your enemies," but that he actually loved his enemies. He lived as if what he said was true and real, and of course, it was. The question is whether we do the same. "You have taken off your old self," Paul tells us, "with its practices and have put on the new self, which is being renewed in knowledge in the image of its Creator" (Colossians 3:9-10).

If we are to live as if that which we uphold as true actually is true, it must be reflected in our public lives, not just our personal lives and relationships. Our lives are not merely private, they are public too. As citizens, our lives are inescapably political.

Here's the thing about spiritual formation for public life: we can count on the Holy Spirit as our helper, just as we can for our "personal" spiritual formation. We can expect to see God working through and in us as we act in public, just as we expect to see the difference Christlikeness makes in our personal lives. Yes, we need to be wary of the pull that politics can have on us, but we should also have the faith to imagine the pull we can have on our politics. If a growing number of Christians decided their faith had implications for their politics, would that not change our politics? Could we not see our politics pulled toward a greater appreciation for human dignity? For justice? For humility? This is spiritual formation for the sake of our neighbors. For too long, we have only asked what politicians must do in order to meet our needs. Now, we must seek to become the kind of people our politics, and our neighbors, need.

Kaitlyn Schiess has returned from a period of thought and study into these complicated dynamics. Imagine that she has just walked into your sanctuary to share with the church what she has learned. Listen carefully.

Apolitical OR Unexamined

WHAT SPIRITUAL FORMATION
HAS TO DO WITH POLITICS

[The church] cannot have an inner life without having at the same time a life which expresses itself outwardly as well. She cannot hear her Lord and not hear the groaning of the Creation.

KARL BARTH

I've spent my entire life in evangelical spaces: I grew up in a variety of evangelical churches as a nomadic military kid, attended a prominent evangelical university, and chose an evangelical seminary. For good or for ill, it wasn't until college that I really knew a world outside of the subculture I'd been raised in. While attending Liberty University, I experienced what I like to call "ideological whiplash." I spent my weekdays studying politics and history in a space still deeply influenced by a particular form of conservative political engagement while my weekends were occupied traveling the country to compete as part of a debate community strongly influenced by the kind of progressive politics my classes condemned. The more I moved back and forth between them, both the conservative and progressive spaces started to look more and more like the caricatures that one side painted of the other. I could see how reactive each side was, how much it defined itself by opposition to the other, and how powerfully it compelled the loyalty of its particular communities. This personal experience prompted my exploration into the history at play here. And by the time the 2016 election was ramping up, many of my classmates and friends were also more closely examining the evangelical legacy we had inherited.

Liberty's founder and first president, Jerry Falwell Sr., was a pastor, televangelist, and the founder of a political advocacy organization called the Moral Majority. The organization was formed in the midst of a theological and political shift among American Protestants toward greater political involvement, often motivated by a perceived sense of moral decay in American culture. The Religious Right, or Christian Right, began to gain influence in the 1980s, and the Moral Majority was one expression of this trend. A variety of explanations exists for this surge in conservative activism among church leaders and lay Christians, but the predominant explanation goes like this: evangelicals were happily apolitical until Roe v. Wade, when, motivated by theological opposition to abortion, they entered into the political world, eventually adding other cultural issues to their platform. Yet historian Randall Balmer calls this the "abortion myth."[1] In reality, the 1974 Internal Revenue Service decision to revoke the tax-exempt status of Bob Jones University, due to their ban on interracial dating, was the primary catalyst. Many private all-white schools or universities (often Christian) that were formed in response to the Brown v. Board of Education decision to desegregate public schools were similarly stripped of their tax-exempt status.[2] Conservative activist Paul Weyrich had tried to get evangelical leaders interested in political activism for years. In the end, Weyrich says that what changed their mind wasn't abortion or school prayer, but tax-exempt status for segregated schools.[3]

Eventually this burgeoning evangelical movement would foster an alliance with Catholics, Jews, and Mormons over a conservative approach to social issues, free market capitalism, and anticommunism.[4] This development is important, as it moved the center of evangelical political energy from a limited focus on a few social issues into a

broader movement based on moral consensus among religious conservatives and a commitment to limited government.[5] The growing
network of theologically conservative churchgoers with newly acquired
conservative political goals prompted an examination of a new voting
bloc, with *Newsweek* declaring 1976 "The Year of the Evangelical."[6]
While the movement seemed to empower Christians who felt their cultural power draining in the wake of the sexual revolution (evangelicals
had "enough votes to run the country,"[7] boasted televangelist Pat Robertson), the alliance would change them as much as they wanted to
change the country. Evangelicals did not gain this sudden rush of political power by focusing on the narrow range of social issues that the
"abortion myth" claims piqued their interest, but by tying their identity
to a larger political movement that would ultimately achieve more
foreign policy and economic goals than the social ones we'd like to
believe began the movement.

Andy Crouch provides a helpful explanation for how the alliance
between religious conservatives and the Republican party became so
unbalanced. Evangelicals who felt their cultural power was waning
sought out a source of power to give them authority again. But the Religious Right would never truly benefit from the deal because, as Crouch
explains, this is how idols work. Idols "work less and less well and they
actually demand more and more of you until eventually, when the idol
has totally taken over your life, it's not giving you anything it promised
at the beginning, and it's asking you to totally abdicate your image-
bearing identity."[8] The social concerns that made evangelicals initially
interested in this alignment have consistently been put on the back
burner in favor of the economic and foreign policy goals that their
support bought for conservative politicians. Evangelicals forged an attachment to a political party that knows it is the beneficiary of a lopsided bargain. Over the course of about twenty years, white American
evangelicals solidified a particular approach to political engagement
largely based in a partnership with the Republican party. This partnership moved from a strategic alliance (we'll support your favored

policies if you support ours) to a single coherence: Christian = Republican. The idol demanded more and more of us until we abdicated our true identities for a false one.

This is the world in which many young Christians grew up—unaware of how exactly we got here, but fully immersed in a religious subculture with strong political elements. And the 2016 election of Donald Trump prompted backlash from young believers precisely because of this subculture.

They felt betrayed by leaders who had touted the importance of the moral character of politicians and deceived when they read the Bible and discovered that conservative economic and foreign policy principles didn't fly off its pages. Younger Christians have never tasted the kind of cultural power that previous generations watched deteriorate. The "culture war" approach is unappealing to a generation thoroughly accustomed to a world that labels their religious beliefs "irrelevant" or "backward." Instead, many are looking for political engagement that wrestles with the difficulty of applying theological convictions to public life and an approach to culture that does more than condemn.

"Too Political"

In response to the backlash from young Christians, and the widespread political division in the church, many public leaders try to avoid the topic of politics entirely. Lobbing a claim of "getting political" communicates that someone is unnecessarily divisive, harboring ulterior motives, or is stepping outside the bounds of their role. After Lysa TerKeurst, president of Proverbs 31 Ministries and a popular speaker and author, visited the White House for a conversation about "families, religious non-profits, and women," she promised her Instagram followers that: "This wasn't a political trip. It was just an everyday gal who loves Jesus being given a seat at the table."[9] We're so averse to the "political" that we'll deny our involvement in it even from one of the greatest seats of political power in the world.

Political is practically a dirty word. It's constantly pitted against the gospel, as if anything political stands in opposition to mere faithful living. We haggle over what counts as a political issue—marking out boundaries that include the issues we'd rather avoid and including all the ones where disagreement won't be tolerated. We even proudly declare issues that require legislative solutions as "not political" when we think they should be supported by everyone. We conflate "political" and "partisan," and we isolate legislative and electoral means of social engagement as the only ones tainted by sin.

Any human system will have its flaws, and no human system should receive our ultimate loyalty. We will be sorely disappointed if we put our hope in fallible and imperfect institutions. Government systems—local or national—suffer the same effects of sin that any other human system does. Instead of isolating them as lower, grungier places of human activity, we should recognize them as spaces to live into our creative capacity as humans.

When I tell new friends that I write about faith and politics, they are almost universally enthusiastic. "Oh, we need Christians doing that!" "Bless your heart, that's important." "What necessary work!" The conversation usually ends there. We all think, in theory, that talking about the relationship between our faith and political participation is important, but very few actually want to have the conversation. We love the *idea* of hard and messy conversations, but we're usually afraid to take the risks involved in actually broaching these topics with the people around us.

Perhaps surprisingly, this impulse toward maligning the political is actually consistent with the political legacy young evangelicals have inherited. The common criticism of the Moral Majority and Religious Right is that it made the Christian faith "too political" by tying our faith to political positions. But perhaps the problem with too closely aligning our faith and a particular strain of conservative politics isn't that the movement was "too political," but that it was actually insufficiently political.

Instead of directly dealing with the complex questions of sorting out what our theological convictions look like in public and seeing our political education as part and parcel of our theological education, we've outsourced. We're afraid of "getting political"—but we aren't afraid of letting others do the "dirty work" for us. Many of our leaders have—implicitly or explicitly—communicated that there are a set of approved conservative sources that will give us the guidance we need—not just in policy details, but in the kind of philosophy that should motivate our participation. That's why the history is important: we solidified a relationship that was meant to be useful to deal with immediate political concerns, but it turned into a dependent relationship on an outside source for education about our ultimate values.

Even when we recognize the role of Christian leaders in guiding our political training, we still place our political education on the shoulders of Christian parachurch organizations. During my time working for a local church, we hosted an event that was advertised as a series of simulcast talks intended to spark conversations about our cultural moment. It was broadcast all over the country, into local churches that were offered simple guidelines on how to host the event. Many of us on staff were excited to introduce the congregation to topics that we knew they would otherwise avoid, like race, economics, and politics. At the end of the night, we realized how misguided our hopes had been. The topics were given none of the necessary introduction, because a nationally simulcast talk couldn't know everyone's background or the contexts they were living in. We had no real strategy for continuing the conversations, and we felt no responsibility to defend anything that might rub up against the political preferences of the congregation, because it wasn't our event. We had no skin in the game.

We wanted to check a box. Political engagement: check. Our fear of "getting political" had landed our congregation in the same spot that the Moral Majority had placed them in: we lacked adequate resources to discern how to politically engage with the world around us.

So, even for those of us weary of a legacy we may have had no part in shaping, the call is clear: we have to get political.

Brains and Bodies

In one of my seminary classes, we had one large project to work on throughout the whole semester: designing a ministry plan, with all the hypothetical details. I decided to create a plan for a church to intentionally introduce political training into the regular life of the church. Part of the project required that we research and select a curriculum. I read the descriptions and table of contents for dozens of curricula, surprised to find an abundance of options. Most of them promised to teach Christians how to "engage the culture" and "change the world." Yet not only did these studies severely limit the scope of necessary political education for Christians, they also almost exclusively focused on explaining the "biblical" position on a select number of issues. Rather than offering a robust theological basis for understanding human government, our obligations to it as strangers and sojourners in this world, and the limitations and possibilities of creative political work, they took a laundry list of current political issues and matched them to Bible verses. Many of the options were commendable, but they shed light on the expectations of most church leaders: hit all the hot-button issues and give us the right answers to a few pressing political problems. If this was all Christians had to guide them, they might know where they should stand on a few policies, but they would have no idea why government exists, what our relationship to it should be, or how to faithfully engage with the sticky political problems of the future. I ended up using this part of my project to explain why an entirely new curriculum needed to be written.

Decades of political disagreement among American Christians should remind us that there's no easy "what the Bible says" about politics, to say nothing about centuries of disagreement among Christians around the world. Even a more comprehensive theological approach will fall flat if it relies exclusively on giving us a new set of facts and beliefs. We're constantly learning more about how embodied our learning and thinking is, and Christians are beginning to connect this scientific research with a truth we've always known: we aren't just "brains on a stick."

Philosopher James K. A. Smith has been credited for a resurgence in evangelical thinking about the "liturgies" that form us—the embodied habits, practices, and corporate pedagogies that we repeatedly participate in. Instead of thinking of humans as primarily thinking beings, he has argued (as Augustine and others before him) that we are primarily loving beings, motivated and driven by the things we have learned to love. Learning is not a purely cognitive process by which we gain information about the things we love and then make logical decisions based on that knowledge. Instead, this learning usually looks more like picking up implicit messages about the "good life" through the things we habitually consume, watch, experience, and rehearse with our bodies.

Smith's paradigm is a helpful lens for looking at the places and habits that are most spiritually formative, and they are often found outside of the church. The contemporary evangelical church has often failed to grasp the formative power of the cultural artifacts we consume and use outside of the church while letting the repeated actions and artifacts inside of the church go largely unexamined. We try to speak to people deeply formed by images, emotions, bodily practices, and ritualistic experiences outside of the church with a set of sermon points to learn. As Smith says, we're "pouring water on our head to put out a fire in our heart."[10]

This lens for looking at the forces that are most spiritually formative (and the necessary counterformative practices) is an approach that we desperately need to use in our conversations about political theology. Other areas of Christian living may require embodied practices that teach us how and what to love, but if politics is that mucky realm we only enter into out of necessity, we're not likely to give it the same level of attention. I've become convinced, however, that one of the most important tasks for the evangelical church in America is to examine our spiritual formation in a political direction. I use that phrase, "spiritual formation in a political direction," in two ways: the ways we are spiritually formed by the political forces around us, and the ways our intentional spiritual formation practices form us in political ways.

The word *direction* is important. We tend to compartmentalize, splitting our theological and political convictions. Instead, both have a moral and spiritual element, and neither are content to stay in their own corners. The ideas we gain in one area have underlying values with their own gravitational pull, breaking out of the boxes we put them in. Political values don't stay political; they become ultimate. We often treat our political convictions as if they operate on a lower rung than our theological convictions. We can value wealth or security on this lower political level while maintaining that on a higher spiritual level we value God's kingdom. But our political tendencies and practices influence more than this lower realm—they inevitably fight for dominance in our lives. The things we do in a voting booth and a church pew alike will shape the values we hold.

These connections between our spiritual formation and our political participation often go unexamined in our churches and communities. In February 2017, a long list of prominent evangelicals signed a joint letter criticizing President Trump's executive order temporarily banning travelers from seven nations, indefinitely ending the acceptance of Syrian refugees, and reducing the total number of refugees to be admitted into the country. Influential conservative leaders like Tim Keller and Ed Stetzer were among the signees.

And yet, just a few weeks after the letter was published, Pew Research released data showing that 76 percent of white evangelicals supported the executive order—evidence of a clear disconnect between the beliefs of many of our leaders and the congregations and communities they lead. That gap reveals the importance of viewing political participation as another area of the life of the whole person that must be nurtured and guided by the church. It shows that we may be woefully unaware of the formative power of political forces, and perhaps most importantly, it shows the weakness of our modern practices to counteract them.

Missing Furniture

When you enter a room in your home, a room that you've likely entered hundreds or thousands of times before, you rarely bump into the furniture. Your brain doesn't even need to take the time to consciously register the locations of the couch or coffee table. Your body knows how to take you through the room on a precognitive level.[11] For example, I recently removed a large bookshelf from the very front of my bedroom. Yet for weeks after I'd done that, I still instinctively entered the room from the far left of the door, farthest from a large obstacle that was no longer there.

It isn't just that our brain sees the furniture and makes a superfast decision to avoid it. We simply don't need to cognitively process the material things around us that we have learned to navigate with our bodies. I could physically feel the presence of a missing bookshelf, and it took weeks for my body to relearn the landscape of the room.

Likewise, we are formed in ways that help us navigate the world, before thinking even enters the picture. In every personality test I've ever taken, I've been labeled a thinker. It takes a lot more energy for me to process emotions than it does for me to evaluate arguments. But even those of us with this particular bent approach the world more emotionally than we think. Rosalind Picard, founder and director of the Affective Computing Lab at MIT, studied the way humans use emotion in processing and decision-making in an effort to see if this affective approach to the world could be used in computing. She explains that humans use emotion to deal with the complexity of life, instances where rational processing takes too much time. In other words, emotion is an "integral component of human decision making."[12]

Not Apolitical, Just Unexamined

We're unaware of the formative power of politics, but we're also unaware of the political force of our spiritual formation practices. Our church services, no matter how "low church" they may be, have regular practices: the way we pray and sing together, the way we practice communion, the order of our services. Our classes and Bible studies also have practices: some of us eat together, others sit in rows of chairs. We segregate by age or gender or marital status. Our everyday lives certainly have practices: we habitually consume media, we regularly drive the same streets and neighborhoods, we water our plants and brush our teeth and unload the dishwasher. No matter how seemingly inconsequential, we have practices that slowly shape us in profound ways. These practices have the potential to counter the political and cultural forces vying for our loyalty, but they also have the potential to reinforce them.

Some definitions are helpful here. I use the phrase "spiritual formation" in much the same way that Smith uses the word *liturgies*. These are not limited to spiritual disciplines or corporate worship but encompass both—and more. We are spiritually formed (for good or ill) by any number of things, but particularly by those things that are repetitive, embodied, and impart a larger meaning. When we use the phrase "spiritual formation" in the church, we usually mean only the intentional practices we participate in with the expressed purpose of becoming more like Christ. But seeing our unintentional practices, too, as spiritually formative is important. I keep that word, *spiritual*, because nothing truly formative can impact us in ways that aren't spiritual.

It's about time we defined *political*. This word primarily indicates government functions—elections, legislation, court decisions, and so on. But delineating what pertains to the government and what doesn't is a messy business. Our common life together will always involve the government in some way. When we wake up in the morning, our eyes open in neighborhoods that are determined by politics. The racial and ethnic makeup of our communities aren't an accident; they are greatly influenced by government decisions about zoning laws and a long history of legal segregation. The schools we attend are also implicated— local and national policies affect the opportunities our neighbors have access to. The stores we shop at are governed by policies that protect or

neglect workers and businesses. The food we buy is influenced by policies that subsidize or regulate food industries. The cars we drive require
gas, an industry with significant political implications for foreign policy
and environmental law.

If we're truly concerned about our neighbors, then we'll inevitably
come into contact with even more political questions. When we work
at a local food pantry, we're working amidst a number of regulations
that determine how nonprofits function. We're interacting with a
problem (poverty) that has varied political causes and solutions. When
we help local refugee children learn English, we're sitting across the
table from children whose lives have been greatly dictated by politics—
the conflicts that harmed them, the way the United States processes
refugees, the number we accept, the benefits they can access. When our
churches support a prison ministry, they are operating in the web of
decades of criminal justice politics. Whether or not we even serve in
any of these capacities is often determined not just by our own preferences but by the politics determining the proximity we have to any of
these marginalized populations. Likewise, when the youth group has
to bus kids to the "other side of the tracks" to find a nonprofit to serve
alongside, that's politics.

Our lived theology has political consequences. Examining the political implications of our practices isn't about shifting the focus away
from God. Our worship—corporately or individually—glorifies him
above all else, and he has made it abundantly clear that the way we
treat other people is a big part of how he views our worship. Isaiah is
worth quoting in full on this subject.

> Hear the word of the Lord,
>   you rulers of Sodom;
> listen to the instruction of our God,
>   you people of Gomorrah!
> "The multitude of your sacrifices—
>   what are they to me?" says the Lord.

"I have more than enough of burnt offerings,
    of rams and the fat of fattened animals;
I have no pleasure
    in the blood of bulls and lambs and goats.
When you come to appear before me,
    who has asked this of you,
        this trampling of my courts?
Stop bringing meaningless offerings!
    Your incense is detestable to me.
New Moons, Sabbaths and convocations—
    I cannot bear your worthless assemblies.
Your New Moon feasts and your appointed festivals
    I hate with all my being.
They have become a burden to me;
    I am weary of bearing them.
When you spread out your hands in prayer,
    I hide my eyes from you;
even when you offer many prayers,
    I am not listening.

Your hands are full of blood!

Wash and make yourselves clean.
    Take your evil deeds out of my sight;
        stop doing wrong.
Learn to do right; seek justice.
    Defend the oppressed.
Take up the cause of the fatherless;
    plead the case of the widow." (Isaiah 1:10-17)

When our spiritual formation practices (the sacrifices and the festivals for Israel, and the spiritual disciplines, sacraments, and worship
services for us) go unexamined, we end up participating in rituals that
are "detestable" and a "burden" to God. Good practices lead us in the
direction of seeking justice and defending the oppressed, goals with
unavoidably political dimensions.

A Return to Analog

In the days and weeks after the 2016 election, nothing was more comforting than my language classes. Most of my classes felt worlds away from the reality of a church willingly used as a political pawn. But studying Greek—the hardest class I was taking—felt strangely comforting. There was a quiet joy running under my heartbreak about the state of the American church, precisely because I was starting to put that adjective before church.

The removal of that adjective reminded me that no matter the state of my faith in my country, a whole world lay outside of it. More than that, there was a long and complicated history beyond it too. The words I was studying—words that had been manipulated and abused by Christian leaders I had been taught to trust—were not theirs. They didn't own these words written miles and centuries away from the Starbucks I studied in, miles and centuries away from the board rooms and debate stages where they were wielded like weapons. These words were ancient, a reminder that my faith transcended my particular time and place.

Outside of political concerns, a lot of young people are starting to find comfort in ancient things, even if "ancient" only means thirty years old. In his book *The Revenge of Analog*, reporter David Sax explains how and why people are increasingly interested in "analog experiences" like writing with pen and paper, reading paper copies of books, listening to records, and using Polaroid-like cameras. In this context, "analog" is anything that isn't digital: it doesn't require a computer to work, and it operates in the physical world. "For increasing numbers of people around the world," he writes, "in nearly every place where digital life has acquired a real and lasting presence, analog is now a conscious choice, requiring a greater cost, both materially and in terms of our time and mental capacity, than the digital default. And yet people increasingly elect it."[13] Sax's description of the pleasure many are finding in returning to analog should ring especially true for those of us with a biblical basis for the goodness and givenness of what our bodies experience: hearing "the luxurious sound of unfolding the Sunday newspaper" or the joy "that comes from seeing your thoughts scratched onto a sheet of paper with the push of a pen."[14] We are hungry for physical experiences and embodied community.

Young Christians, often maligned for wanting flashy and new, sometimes get the blame for sleek church buildings, the influx of lasers and fog machines in worship services, and podcasts or livestreams replacing live church attendance. This criticism isn't entirely unfounded, but it's worth asking if maybe young Christians are being given what someone else *thinks* they want.

According to Pew Research, Millennials and Gen Xers are more curious about historic Christian practices than previous generations.[15] While much has been made about the mass exodus of young Christians from the church, nearly as much has been made about their conversion to Anglicanism, Catholicism, or Eastern Orthodoxy. Anecdotal examples abound, with leaders noticing that among the young people staying in the church there is an increased desire for liturgical traditions.[16] Anglican bishop Todd Hunter, who writes of his own journey to a liturgical expression of worship, notes that Christians are searching for historical connectedness, for theology and practices that are not "tied to the whims of contemporary culture but to apostolic-era understandings of Christian faith and practice."[17]

In my own experience attending an evangelical university, I knew many students who moved to more liturgical churches as well as several churches that began adopting more liturgical practices, even in small doses. While the youth groups I grew up in seemed to operate largely on the principle that students thought church was stuffy and boring and needed to be amped up with more modern elements, the real surprise came in college, with so many of us finally getting what we had been implicitly told we wanted for so long—churches and campus worship services that served lattes and used fog machines—and yet we found ourselves *less* satisfied. It seemed that we (young Christians and everyone else) might not have known what we most desperately needed: a return to analog.

The only thing that can truly counter the strength of powerfully formative forces around us is rediscovering rather ancient ideas about
spiritual formation. They're important in so many ways we'll discover,
but this is a foundational one: they require our attention. Unlike many
of our modern rituals, we call them what they are—rituals. Some of our
discomfort with historic Christian traditions may lie in a fear of "ritual"
as mindless, "vain repetitions" (Matthew 6:7 KJV). Yet we can be painfully unaware of how ritualistic our own services already are. Most of
us follow the same order of service, sing many of the same songs, and
pray with a "script" of language that we put in different orders for "spon-
taneous" prayer. We aren't participating in fewer rituals or liturgies,
we're just less aware of them—and that can make them more dangerous.

Many church leaders know that their congregations are being
strongly formed by political forces outside of their reach, but they don't
know what to do. My hope is to offer a way forward—but not a new one.
Maybe one of the best things for evangelicals desperate for an alternative to the political legacies of their elders is to hear this: the way
forward requires looking back.

The Right Question

A friend of mine shared a link to an article about evangelicals' opposition to the United States accepting refugees with the comment, "Do
they not know what their Bible says, or do they not care?" This kind of
bewilderment characterizes many of our conversations about politics,
leaving us to ask, Are we reading the same Bible?

I love my friend's question because it displays the exact misunderstanding I want to dive into. Why do we think/believe/support the
things we do when we have every biblical basis not to? This is a question
that will far outlast any political or cultural moment, and I think the
answer is found in spiritual formation. We evaluate the effects of our
spiritual formation on any number of things, but we primarily look at
our personal piety and ask ourselves: Am I a better person? Do I feel
closer to God? A better question is this: What am I being formed to love?

And the question I'm particularly interested in is this one: How does this practice form me in ways that have consequences for how I treat my neighbor, sometimes through my political participation?

This question will require that we evaluate the world around us, looking beyond the facts and figures we're asked to accept and instead looking at the "liturgies" we're unintentionally participating in, the spiritual formation practices we're uncritically allowing to shape us. We'll have to elevate the significance of things that seem small, zooming in with a microscope to see the ways they're forming us. This connection—between spiritual formation and political practice—is crucial for understanding how we are politically formed in spiritual directions and how we are spiritually formed in political directions. I don't think the question is whether we don't know what our Bible says or that we don't care. The real question is, What is forming us?

THE Liturgy OF Politics

LOVES AND LOYALTIES

Before and beneath governmental politics lie the identities and worldviews of the citizenry. Even the most powerful politician cannot pursue a policy the citizens cannot imagine.

ROBERT WEBBER AND RODNEY CLAPP

When I was a senior at Liberty University, US senator and 2016 presidential hopeful Bernie Sanders came to speak to the largely conservative student body. Liberty had hosted other 2016 candidates during the primaries and was obligated to extend that invitation to any candidate if the university chose to allow any of them to speak. While the campus was not the kind of place you were likely to find support for his politics, Sanders tried to appeal to a shared desire to help the poor, even if many in the audience had different ideas about how to address that problem. To his credit, he entered a pretty unfriendly place to his belief system and tried to find common ground with us. In spite of his very general plea to cooperate on our shared concern for the vulnerable in society, most of the students responded with silence and crossed arms.

It was less than six months later that prominent Christian writer and speaker Ann Voskamp came to speak, using the story of Esther to encourage students to use their power and privilege to advocate for those "outside of the gate." While Voskamp's invitation and arrival were welcomed by students, by the end of her message, the responses were remarkably similar. Some students would later claim that their issue wasn't with her message itself but with an illustration in which she poured a bottle of water on the stage, potentially damaging music equipment. Many of the remarks I heard, however, were about how nice her clothes were, how judged students felt, and how the concepts of privilege and power imbalances were wrong or inappropriate.

When Sanders came to speak, many students responded with the oft-repeated argument: "Caring for the poor is a job for the church, not the government!" Their issue was not ostensibly with his care for the poor and marginalized but with his methods. But Voskamp's message, which completely avoided large-scale political solutions to the problems of poverty and injustice, was met with similar discomfort. Our views on poverty itself, not just economic philosophies or political strategies for addressing it, seemed to have been shaped primarily by our political convictions. A regular diet of Republican politicians and political commentators had done more than educate us about conservative economic philosophy—a larger system of values, loves, and frameworks for the world had snuck in under the surface of these supposedly faith-neutral political beliefs.

The Pull of Politics

It'd be easy to dismiss this as the unfortunate mixing of political partisanship with the passion and relative ignorance of college students, but the impulse illustrated here—"political" opinions that end up shaping the more fundamental theological and moral beliefs we hold—is a universal one. The line between our political beliefs, our moral beliefs, and our theological beliefs is blurry, if not entirely invented. We certainly interact with various people, communities, and institutions in different ways, but none of our beliefs in these categories are ever content to stay in the boxes we've prescribed for them. They'll wander, bleed over, and most importantly, they will seek supremacy. If we aren't aware of the deep pull of these beliefs, we will carelessly incorporate them into our lives, without ordering them, testing them against more foundational beliefs, and putting them in proper submission to the ultimate, controlling authority in our lives.

In his book *Awaiting the King: Reforming Public Theology*, philosopher James K. A. Smith argues that the distinction that we make between ultimate and penultimate values—the eternal/moral/theological values that we hold as ultimate, and the temporal/earthly/pragmatic values that we hold as a means to the end of the ultimate values—is a distinction that is frequently blurred. This is the same distinction we students were making when we thought that we could be uncritically immersed in a particular strand and form of conservative economic policy that we agreed with insofar as it ordered this temporal world, while maintaining moral or theological values that honored the poor and marginalized. In other words, we thought we could enthusiastically consume political content that argued against an extensive welfare system but that we would be unaffected by underlying beliefs that the poor were responsible for their own misfortune, wealth was a sign of righteousness, and poverty was immoral.[1] As Smith says, "the ultimate/ penultimate distinction is not the happy division of labor we imagine, mostly because the political is not content to remain penultimate."[2]

Western Christians have been deeply formed by the political philosophy of liberalism, which Smith says prides itself on "its politics of penultimacy"[3]—posing as a system that not only allows people from different moral and theological backgrounds to work together on penultimate goals, but as an ideology that insulates citizens from the deeper values of those with whom we want to collaborate. Instead, Smith argues that we are inevitably formed by the ultimate values of both the systems we participate in and the people we collaborate with on more temporal goals. Rather than being merely formed by the top-level belief systems we agree with, we are formed all the way down. We cannot truly insulate ourselves from being formed by both the particular political goals we agree with and the underpinnings of such goals. Political projects have a teleology—they are moving in the direction of a certain view of what the world should be like, how humans should act, and good goals we should be working toward. We are wrong to assume that we can go unaffected by the teleological pull of the political projects we participate in.

Another related consequence of our liberal formation is that we tend to view the world as bifurcated along particular lines: civil and religious, moral and political, earthly and eternal. Each of these distinctions certainly has a degree of validity, but nothing in our lives fits neatly in a single category. We fight for political protections for religious freedom, our moral beliefs about the sanctity of life inform our political stances, and our eternal perspective informs the way we live our lives on earth.

Our faith is not a private expression of belief that we leave behind when we enter the public square. We need to unlearn our bent toward a private religion and a public politics—and see our participation in political life as a reflection of our very public faith. We need to understand that our political participation is just as formative as the more "spiritual" activities we participate in individually or communally.

Our Political Loves

Everything we do and every institution we participate in has an effect on our spiritual lives, because no part of our life is separated into spiritual and nonspiritual. But our political participation has an especially strong effect—not just because political projects have that teleological pull, but because of the unique way we participate in them and the level on which they communicate meaning and truth. We'll use the language of rituals to describe the way we engage politically. Rituals are any action we do repeatedly for a reason that has more meaning than the action itself. They don't exist in a vacuum: they exist in a constellation of forces that provide meaning and significance to the actions themselves and determine the possibility of that action.

For example, brushing your teeth might seem like an inconsequential action, but it exists within a particular context: a world with medical knowledge about dental health, the belief that physical health is a universal good, and the technology (a toothbrush, toothpaste) to seek that good. You might have learned all of these things in a cognitive way (reading a children's book about brushing your teeth or listening to your parent or kindergarten teacher explain why brushing is important), but you probably learned this more by brushing your teeth for most of your life. If a scientific article came out today arguing that brushing your teeth is an old-fashioned practice that doesn't actually provide the benefits we were taught, it would probably take a while for you to believe it (or to stop brushing your teeth). Your cognitive knowledge of the supposed insignificance of brushing your teeth would be fighting against the deeply ingrained and bodily knowledge you had of brushing your teeth twice a day for decades.

And yet brushing your teeth is a relatively weak (what Smith calls a "thin"[4]) ritual. It might take a while for you to stop doing it, but you would probably eventually stop doing it. Other rituals are stronger ("thicker") and much more resistant to the introduction of new information that challenges their truth claims.

Our political participation is full of strong rituals—rituals that speak to us on a deeper affective level than dental health. Theologians Robert Webber and Rodney Clapp call this "depth politics"[5]—beneath the outward expressions of political work lie the operating philosophies that form people's identities and loyalties toward a particular view of the world and a standard of goodness. This is true of almost all forms of political participation: our media consumption habits, political discussions online and in person, political rallies or campaign events, or watching sports or entertainment with political messaging. These rituals are robust practices of instilling values and communicating ideas on an affective level. Combine that with a strong teleological pull and you have a powerful set of practices that teach us who or what to fear, who or what to respect, and who "our people" are. In other words, they form our loves and our loyalties.

Our media consumption habits are probably the greatest example of this—while the news has never been devoid of bias and really can't be, most of our television and internet media are able to use video and audio in ways that speak to us on a much more affective level than was possible in the past. Much of the information that sticks in our brains is not propositional information—for example, the annual cost of Medicare, the number of civilians who died in a drone strike, or the exact words the president used to describe his opponent—but the affective information (outrage, fear, joy, hope, or love) that exists within a story to present narratives such as the government is the bad guy who takes away our rights, the terrorists hate our freedom, and strong leaders don't mince words. We may not have any context for whether the annual cost of Medicare is high or low, but the music was harrowing, the commentators were livid, and the story of government overreach is a familiar one.

To be clear: affective information is still information. This is not an argument about how emotions are messy and wrong, while facts are reliable and objective. Affective information is useful, and it's the first resource that humans go to when they have to make decisions quickly. Because we constantly place it in opposition to facts, instead of in opposition to propositional information, we both devalue it and ignore its effects in our lives. Most of us would be uncomfortable admitting we remembered the emotions and storytelling of a news report better than we remembered the propositional information, but we shouldn't be— it's the way humans commonly process information and make sense of a complicated world.

When I was in a particularly difficult semester of seminary, I discovered that the best way to get ready to tackle a long study session was to get a cup of coffee, set up all my books and notes, and watch an inspirational movie trailer. I had learned that the easiest way to get excited about my homework was to remind myself why I was doing it, and the easiest way to do that was by watching a trailer where a woman overcame some obstacle to flourish in a male-dominated field. Very often, this was the movie trailer for the 2019 film *On the Basis of Sex*. The film is a snapshot of the life of Supreme Court justice Ruth Bader Ginsburg and her crusade against laws that discriminated on the basis of sex. While I was inspired by the propositional information—how hard Ginsburg worked in law school, her smart legal arguments, the reality that these laws were ruled unconstitutional—it wasn't the reason I watched the trailer dozens of times that semester.

If all I needed was a reminder of the propositional information, I could have listed it all on a sticky note on my laptop. I watched the trailer for the affective impression it left on me. I identified with the defiant Ginsburg asking questions in a classroom full of men. I found strength from the intent expression on her face as she stood before unfriendly federal judges. And most of all, I found myself working with greater purpose after watching the moment when her tearful daughter asks of Ginsburg's life's work fighting discrimination, "Who was it for, if not for me?"[6]

Was I really processing all of the legal arguments at play in this film? Did I logically deduce the value of women's rights from propositional arguments explained by the actors? Of course not. And neither does that make wrong the conclusions I drew from the movie: women faced and still face legal, political, and social obstacles in America and that it is just to remove them. The problem is not that we are deeply formed by affective communication but that we rarely acknowledge this power or consider what sources we want to be formed by.

This is true of all film, television, and digital media—they operate on an affective register and communicate meaning in a nonpropositional way. But our political participation infuses these sources of information with both a teleological pull and total saturation of message. We find particular political messages, like the four we'll explore in the next chapter, communicated over and over and over again. We find the same few themes running through movies, news broadcasts, football games, TV shows, and holiday celebrations.

And because to a certain extent we choose the media we consume, we contribute to the repetition of certain perspectives. Most people have repeated viewing practices: we choose our news sources based on political loyalties that are then reinforced by those choices, and these sources use powerful combinations of images and language to instill their values in us. Much like the devotion believers have to their local churches, we repeatedly return to the same news sources to find the answers to life's complicated questions, comfort in the face of an uncertain world, and a community that promises us a sense of belonging if we stick with them.

Similarly, our political rallies use rituals, music, and consistent communication about hope in some higher power (be it the power of the human spirit, the American dream, or the modern economy) in ways that look suspiciously like church services. We file into arenas or line the sidewalks where politicians are speaking, crowding in not only to learn from their wisdom, but to express our support of their messages with our bodies and voices. We are moved by the air of possibility, the solidarity with other believers, and the sights and sounds that remind us we are part of a larger story.

We might think that we make political decisions based on propositional information, but we are overwhelmingly motivated by our loves and our loyalties. What have we been taught to love, value, and respect? What ideas, people, or institutions have we been taught to be loyal to? When we watch a campaign ad or a newscast, the combination of images and sounds combine to provoke emotional, sometimes visceral responses from us. We don't just take in information about immigration or healthcare; we learn who or what to fear or love. We are trained in these emotional responses by the rituals in which we participate.

The Framework of Loyalty

Our political participation usually operates on the level of our loves. We are pulled toward a particular set of goods. We are motivated by the people, society, culture, and ultimate values that we have been taught to love. But there's also a second element that gives political participation such a strong formative effect in our lives: the framework of loyalty.

As Rosalind Picard's work with the Affective Computing Lab at MIT shows, as explained in the last chapter, humans don't always deal with complexity well. We live in a world with a lot of detailed information and very few resources to deal with it. We find ways of quickly sorting and processing that information. One key way we do this is by sorting people into categories—"my people" and "other people" being the most foundational distinction. Social psychologist Christena Cleveland explains that one way we conserve our limited cognitive energy is by choosing what information we'll pay attention to, using the mental shortcut of categorizing people and avoiding the kind of information that would demand more cognitive resources to sort through.[7] We use our categories when we want to quickly evaluate the value of a media source (Are they on my team?), a commentator (Is he or she one of us?), or the personality at the center of a story (Is he or she like me?).

The fundamental framework of our political liturgies is loyalty—who do you belong to and who belongs to you? It is a basic human instinct and a good, God-given thing to identify with a community. In fact, submitting to a human community that offers rules of engagement—language to communicate with, ideas that ground your life, and boundaries that you stay within—is how the church works. Christians don't exist in a vacuum; we both participate in and submit to our local community of believers and to larger Christian tradition and history as sources of authority in our lives. We also live as active participants in that community when we challenge accepted norms that don't find their basis in Scripture. That is rightly placed loyalty: finding the sources of community, authority, and meaning in the Christian community that God has given as a gift to us and commanded that we participate in as a gift to the world.

Our national identities, racial or ethnic communities, and our smaller local affiliations all demand a certain kind of loyalty from us. Yet those loyalties are only rightly placed when they find their context and meaning in light of the ultimate loyalty we have to the body of Christ. It's important to note that this will look different depending on the particulars. A white person's loyalty to their racial community must be entirely discarded when placed in light of the loyalty they have to the people of God—a people that include those marginalized and oppressed because of white supremacy. A black person's loyalty to their racial community may be strengthened by their loyalty to the people of God, as they appreciate the prophetic witness of the black church in America and find refuge in their particular community. It is not that every other identity or loyalty we have is ordered under this larger one in the same exact way, but rather that our ultimate loyalty to the body of Christ informs and shapes those other loyalties, sometimes in different ways.

Misplaced loyalties are powerful and dangerous forces precisely because they play on our desire to join a community and submit to its authority. When we do this, we don't need to read an opposing opinion because our community has already ruled it suspect. We don't have to engage with those we disagree with because they aren't part of "us." We don't need to evaluate the merits of a particular policy because the "other side" proposed it.

This impulse is not altogether wrong: Christians are called to live as members of a community that has authority over us, and our community gives context and meaning to the information we have to process in the world. That's why the logic and framework of loyalty is especially powerful. It's also why it is so important that our loyalties not get confused or disordered.

The 2016 presidential election is a good example of this. Over the course of the election, many Republican politicians, pundits, and voters moved from rejecting Donald Trump outright, to cautiously tolerating him, to enthusiastically supporting him. Some of this progression was due to the sense of loyalty that many had to the Republican party. Some of it was due to the loyalty that many felt to particular policies such as abortion and religious freedom. Some of it was due to the loyalty that many felt to their nation in the form of supporting Trump's immigration and foreign policy proposals. Whatever the form of loyalty, the drastic shift that many conservative voters, commentators, and institutions underwent is not explainable merely by shifting political circumstances. Something stronger than logical propositions was going on.

Humans are always looking for belonging and meaning—two things that communities give us. Our performance of loyalty reinforces our membership in that community—we legitimize ourselves as members in a community when we display our loyalty to those outside it. This is why congresspeople will use their loyalty to their party or its leader as a selling point in campaign ads. It communicates to voters that this person is committed to the same community as them, that they are willing to do what it takes to get the community's goals accomplished, and that they are one of them. If a political leader's credentials are threatened, it's easier to fall back on loyalty or to contrast their devotion with an inconsistent opponent.

Political participation inevitably involves a certain degree of loyalty: to ideas or policies, to political parties, and to the nation in which we are political participants. Everyone will make decisions about what ideas or policies they will support, and everyone finds themselves with certain obligations to the country they live in. And yet the very nature of loyalty—the way it helps us quickly categorize people and make decisions about complex issues—makes it a powerful force in our lives.

The Language of Fear

I was a competitive debater in college. Contrary to popular perception, policy debate is rarely about rhetorical skill or presentation. It is all about information, logic, and speed. We would spit out as many policy details as we could in a single breath before taking a giant gulp of air and beginning again. We wrote the other team's arguments down on long sheets of legal-sized paper and lined up our responses, attacking their evidence and the structure of their argument. It was fast-paced, technical, and always ended in nuclear war.

It didn't matter if the topic was an international peace treaty or minor regulatory changes for offshore windmills, everything always ended in nuclear war.[8] It didn't start there, of course. An economic downturn or a skirmish between two nations as a result of the proposed policy would spiral into greater chaos and conflict until it resulted in ultimate destruction. It wasn't always like that (and it has shifted away from this a bit since I was in college). In earlier years of collegiate debate, economic decline and regional war could be pitted against each other as reasonably important impacts. But once one team decided to raise the stakes to the point of global annihilation, there was no looking back. The only way to beat a nuclear war is to threaten one of your own.

If loyalty is the primary framework of political participation, fear is the primary language. While people are often motivated by particular concepts of flourishing—James K. A. Smith identifies these as visions of the "good life"[9]—an easier way of communicating those concepts is by painting a scary picture. Fear is a powerful motivator, whether it be fear of a future cataclysmic event, of the "bad guys," or of what society will become.

Fear is also fundamentally antisocial. Our fear causes us to protect ourselves above the common good of a community. Adam and Eve hid in the garden for fear of God instead of entering into reconciliatory community with him. Peter denied his relationship with Jesus (and solidarity with him in his suffering) out of fear. Esther battled fear that would have prompted her to protect herself instead of standing with her community.

Philosopher Martha Nussbaum has studied the role that fear plays in our political process and describes how fear drives out all thoughts of other people, prioritizing the safety and security of the individual: "Soldiers describe the experience of fear in combat as involving a vivid inward focus on their whole body, which becomes their whole world. (This is why military training has to focus so obsessively on building team loyalty—because it has to counter a deep contrary tendency.)"[10] She points out that in the face of a physical threat like assault or a dire medical diagnosis, we may fear for our loved ones, but this is just an indicator that our sense of self has enlarged to include these people. This dynamic poses important questions for Christians: What sense of self are we cultivating? Where have we learned to draw the circle of self whose interests we consider in times of crisis? Does our circle of self include those in our local community, nation, or the body of Christ?

Politicians and political practitioners know that fear is powerful and motivating. "Fear is easy," says Rick Wilson, a Florida-based Republican ad maker.[11] "You associate your opponent with terror, with fear, with crime, with causing pain and uncertainty." In 2002, Wilson made an ad criticizing Democratic Senator Max Cleland (a veteran who lost three limbs in Vietnam) by visually associating him with images of terrorists Saddam Hussein and Osama bin Laden.[12]

Fear operates on an affective level, provoking responses that go against our cognitively held ideals. Fear is such an exceptionally effective motivator that it can even sway people against their preexisting political loyalties (especially impressive, when you remember how strong our sense of loyalty is!). Some political scientists have credited fear of terrorism for some of the GOP's success in elections following the September 11 attacks. Political scientist Shana Gadarian argues that evidence from the 2002 and 2004 elections show that concern about terrorism was a strong predictor of voter's decisions.[13]

On the other side, and broadly speaking, Democrats use fear on other issues, such as the effects of global climate change and the medical costs of changing healthcare policy. The fact that fear is a strong motivator does not mean that these are not real issues with serious effects that should concern us, but it does mean that we have to understand the deep effect it can have on us psychologically and spiritually.

Political participation requires motivating people: to vote, campaign, donate, support, and elect. A powerful tool at the disposal of political forces for this participation, likewise, is fear. Legitimate issues such as terrorism, climate change, and healthcare are turned into looming threats with catastrophic consequences that can only be averted by the heroine or hero with the salvific political solution. The issue is boiled down to its scariest elements, and the threat is exaggerated to the point where any solution at all should be accepted, since the consequences of inaction are shown to be so severe.

Fear is an embodied experience, prompting physical and psychological responses to perceived threats, and is easily communicated in a nonpropositional way, as campaign ads combine the words of a politician with frightening images and sounds. Our bodies are wired to respond to threats in self-protection (normally a good thing), and that can easily become a useful political tool. It's no wonder then that so much Scripture is devoted to fighting fear, not merely for the personal inner peace we can gain but for the sake of the community around us. Our fear easily isolates and pits us against each other in a contest for security and safety, and God continually commands us not to fear but to trust in Him, the Creator and sustainer of the community into which we were called.

Idolatry

There's one element of political participation's strong pull that does get a lot of airtime: idolatry. Christians tend to apply the language of idolatry to every area of our lives. Yet our habit of identifying anything from chocolate chip cookies to football teams as idols lessens the impact of the real meaning of the word. In Scripture, Israel is repeatedly judged for her idolatry, worshiping worthless objects instead of the one true God. But the prophets who so consistently communicate this judgment don't describe her idolatry as merely misplaced valuing of some good thing (the way we often use the term), but as capitulation to a different story and set of values. Idols make promises of protection and provision, and they require allegiance. Their worshipers don't merely love them too much; they submit to these idols and worship them.

While our relationships to chocolate chip cookies and football teams can certainly dishonor God, perhaps we've watered down the language of idolatry to the point where we miss the real idols. Political participation has a unique ability to inspire idolatry in people precisely because it so often involves promises of protection and provision, requires sacrifices, legitimizes authority, and inspires submission and worship. American Christians' alignment with the Republican party became an idol because it made promises of protection, required sacrifices to be able to continue to make those promises, and worked less and less well at fulfilling them over time as the hold it held over Christians became stronger.[14] The myth of the Religious Right is that Christians are in control of their political alliance, using the voting power they possess to achieve their own ends. Over time, this idol did what all idols do: it took control, demanding more and more from its worshipers in exchange for less and less of what they want.

In their book *Hope in Troubled Times: A New Vision for Confronting Global Crises*, Bob Goudzwaard, Mark Vander Vennen, and David Van Heemst explain this concept in the context of weapons acquisition during the Cold War: "The final stage of idol worship—the role reversal of idol and idol worshipper—was therefore present. This reversal indicated that the range of the ideology was absolute. Though initially we thought ourselves able to use and control weapons technology, the reality was that increasingly it controlled us. . . . A god arose, and fear and hypnosis were its tools of terror."[15] Idols are not merely things that we love more than we should: they are able to control us and motivate our actions. We end up serving the very things we thought were serving us.

The prophets repeatedly proclaim God's judgment on Israel for two sins: idolatry and social injustice. These two sins are intimately related, for as Israel moves away from God as their source of protection and provision, they seek it elsewhere, in idols that promise what they cannot provide. The only way idols can continue to make these promises is by asking from their worshipers what those followers can only get by exploiting other people. In ancient Israel, the idols of wood and stone often required child sacrifice, and idolatrous alliances with foreign nations required reliance upon shaky treaties with untrustworthy partners. Our idols of power, privilege, and wealth will ask us to gain power we can't get without taking it from other people, privilege we can't gain without exploiting other people, and wealth we can't gain without stealing it from others. Our political participation is at unique risk of idolization precisely because it is so tangled up with these idols.

There's a reason in Scripture that idolatry is a national issue for Israel. Rarely about an individual, idolatry implicates the entire community. Our loves—our relationships, hobbies, or earthly pleasures—may be disordered, but they more often turn into worship when we gather in communities that love the same thing, seek comfort or security in the stories they tell, and engage in communal rituals of worship. Dallas Cowboys fans may know lots of information about the team, but their love is nurtured and expanded when they go to a game, dressed in the right identity-declaring colors, surrounded by other fans, chanting the same words, and participating in the ritual of the game.

As James K. A. Smith describes, "liturgies—whether 'sacred' or 'secular'—shape and constitute our identities by forming our most fundamental desires and our most basic attunement to the world."[16] The strongest forces in our lives are not the kind of propositional truths we can write on a sticky note and cognitively affirm, but the bodily rituals we participate in, the stories we tell and live into, and the communities that give us belonging and meaning.

The Tension of Formative Spaces

Football games are not bad in themselves. They're opportunities to participate in God's good gift of human creativity, but they can go awry because of their religious nature. The same can be said of political engagement. Government is a God-ordained human institution that evidences the creativity he gave his creatures and the command he gave in the garden to rule, reign, and steward his good creation. Just like all human creative effort, however, politics is subject to the effects of sin in the world whereby God's good gifts become perverted and corrupted.

If our response to the powerful nature of these experiences (what Smith calls "liturgies") is to rid our lives and churches of them, we will fall into another pitfall: shirking the responsibility God gave humanity to steward his creation and the command God gave the church to live for the sake of the world. In other words, if we avoided everything that has formative power in our lives, we wouldn't do anything. Our educational institutions are formative spaces, our workplaces are formative spaces, our places of entertainment and commerce are formative spaces.

This is the tension that we live in as we make our way in a world that God created good and sin has corrupted: humans were made to creatively and authoritatively work and play on this earth, and yet our work and play is never without the effects of sin. Our response to these liturgies should not be avoidance or total rejection but careful engagement and productive criticism.

3

OF THIS **World**

THE GOSPELS OF PROSPERITY, PATRIOTISM, SECURITY, AND SUPREMACY

"Merely" political and social allegiances trump religious
allegiances all the time, whether in presidential primaries,
under the grotesque shadow of the lynching tree, or in
horrifying cases like the Rwandan genocide.

JAMES K. A. SMITH

We all live in light of some gospel or other—the good news that while we suffer from a fundamental problem with the world, salvation is possible if we submit to a new ruler of our lives and become part of a new people. Our gospels each have their own creation or origin stories, a "fall" where evil enters those stories, and the promise of salvation in someone or something. Some of us whose lives are shaped by the Christian gospel are also influenced by other gospels—stories about what's really wrong with the world and the salvific solution to the problem.

I can no longer go to a shopping mall without thinking about James K. A. Smith's explanation of the liturgy of a shopping mall. When you walk into a mall, you are immersed in the sights, sounds, and smells of a particular story about the world. This story begins with humanity created good—beautiful, flawless, perfectly clothed and perfumed—but corrupted by poverty and ugliness. Salvation is found in acquiring the goods that will turn you into the person the ads and mannequins portray: happy, sexy, wealthy. Ask Nordstrom into your heart and your sins of deficiency will be forgiven.

This consumerism is certainly a gospel we easily allow to define our lives, but there are a few particularly political gospels that American Christians have allowed to overshadow the true gospel of Jesus Christ. These are the gospels of prosperity, patriotism, security, and supremacy, yet this is by no means an exhaustive list. These are also all historically and culturally contingent—they reflect neither all American Christians (especially nonwhite American Christians) nor every moment in American or Christian history. Each of these gospels overlaps the others in certain places and have more specific manifestations in different times and places as well. These are merely a few helpful concepts for understanding the many competing gospels in which we are immersed and where these gospels bump up against the true gospel.

The Prosperity Gospel

Many evangelical Christians don't mind yelling "Prosperity gospel!" in a crowded room. We are incredibly adept at recognizing its most obvious form: a slick preacher with designer suits and a couple jets promising that God will return your "seed money" tenfold if you have enough faith. We derogatorily refer to this as the "health and wealth" or "name it and claim it" gospel, or more politely as the Word of Faith movement. Yet many of us who would turn up our noses at the prosperity gospel in these more garish manifestations might be discomforted to discover just how much of this message we've likely accepted.

Kate Bowler, assistant professor of the history of Christianity in North America at Duke Divinity School, literally wrote the book on the prosperity gospel. *Blessed: A History of the American Prosperity Gospel* was the result of ten years researching the preachers, churches, and networks that preach that God promises health and financial prosperity to the faithful. But when Bowler was diagnosed with stage IV cancer at age thirty-five, she realized just how much she had subconsciously believed the gospel she had devoted years to understanding as a supposed outsider.

Traveling the world to study the movement, she had never believed the preachers who claimed God promised healing to his children, but when she herself became sick, it seemed an act of cosmic injustice. You can reject the explicit form of the prosperity gospel and still believe on some level that God rewards good behavior in the form of healthy bodies and hefty bank accounts. The shiny exterior of the prosperity gospel is the "name it and claim it" proclamations, but a more pervasive reality underlies it. Bowler explains it this way: "The movement has perfected a rarefied form of America's addiction to self-rule, which denies much of our humanity: our fragile bodies, our finitude, our need to stare down our deaths (at least once in a while) and be filled with dread and wonder."[1]

Many American Christians have unwittingly accepted the belief that we are in control of our lives, particularly our financial futures. We have accepted the gospel of the free market, trusting that a capitalist society will reward those who work hard. Even if we recognize the frailty of our bodies, we rarely recognize the fragility of our finances. God might not guarantee good health to the faithful, but the free market guarantees success to the hardworking. Which necessarily means that if you are not successful—if your business fails, you lose your job, or your bills pile up—you are at fault and your failure is a moral one: America rewards the righteous with wealth, and your poverty is a result of your sin.

Like all gospels, the prosperity gospel is communicated more powerfully through stories than propositional truths. The phrase "rags to riches" comes from Horatio Alger's dime novels in the mid-nineteenth century where each of these stories center around a teenage boy who, through hard work and determination, overcomes his unfortunate circumstances and achieves success and wealth. From early in our country's history, these stories infiltrated our collective consciousness to make us believe that opportunities for success and wealth are available to all and guaranteed to the righteous.

In the early twentieth century, advertisements began to tell these stories with particular flair. Historian Roland Marchand describes these ads as "dramatizing the American dream and giving it pictorial form"[2] — in other words, selling a visual representation of the good life that Americans believed was due to those who worked hard and had faith in America. Perhaps most telling, Marchand describes a few particular narratives in this kind of advertising as "parables."[3]

Today, we eat up the same stories in the form of advertisements. Rags-to-riches stories get told in viral video clips where strangers or bosses reward hardworking employees, in films like *The Pursuit of Happyness* or *The Blind Side*, or on reality TV shows like *American Idol* or *Shark Tank*. The story is pretty much the same: a hardworking and deserving person gains success by beating the system or earning the favor of someone powerful. We rarely question the injustice inherent in the circumstances of these stories or recognize how rare they really are. We're too caught up in a familiar and comforting story that promises prosperity if we play by the rules.

Bowler notes that the prosperity gospel in its traditional form and civil religion in America share strikingly similar qualities. Both take foundational American characteristics and sacralize them: while civil religion deifies the founding of the United States (the next gospel we'll look at), the prosperity gospel deifies the American Dream of "upward mobility, accumulation, hard work, and moral fiber."[4] It places great weight on individuals to chart their own paths, make their own destinies, and take control of their own resources—and then puts moral weight on their ability to succeed.

Not too many of us would admit this outright, but our mental pictures of the poor and the wealthy come with moral connotations. On some level, the story of the American Dream has wriggled its way under our skin, teaching us to expect that financially successful people must have done something *right*. Dr. David Innes, professor of politics at The King's College in New York City, and author and activist Lisa Sharon Harper authored *Left, Right & Christ: Evangelical Faith in Politics* in 2011, a book of political dialogue from two different perspectives. They also wrote a series of *Huffington Post* articles responding to questions based on pertinent social issues. One of these articles had the two answer the question, "Is the American dream God's dream?" Neither writer responded with an enthusiastic affirmation, but Dr. Innes's answer is an illuminating example of the way moral judgments show up in our descriptions of wealth and poverty.

> The American Dream is generally associated with social and economic rising with a view generally to modest suburban comfort. You arrive with a cardboard suitcase and three dollars in your pocket and you end up with a thriving business. You start out sharing a bedroom with three brothers in the moral squalor of a Brooklyn tenement and you end up with a big backyard and a pool on middle-class Long Island. With hard work and opportunity, you can make it here. The American Dream.[5]

Dr. Innes is not answering the question yet. He's merely defining the terms. But notice the moral language that has slipped in here: the poverty associated with a cardboard suitcase and sharing a bedroom with three brothers occurs in the context of "moral squalor." This is contrasted with "a big backyard and a pool on middle-class Long Island." Most of us—especially those of us who grew up in relative wealth—might skip right past the moral judgment made there, but it's incredibly important. What makes a Brooklyn tenement less moral than a big backyard in Long Island?

Our mental picture of a cramped bedroom occupied by people with three dollars in their pockets comes with stereotypical connotations of drug abuse, sexual immorality, and crime; middle-class backyards conjure up a picture of wholesome nuclear families, hardworking parents, and well-behaved children. Few would seriously argue that those pictures accurately represent reality, but they haunt our understandings of wealth and poverty.

Why do we assume that there's anything better about the kinds of immorality, crime, and thievery that more commonly occur in wealthier areas? We have just as much reason to associate wealth with shady business deals, mistreating or exploiting people, and sexual immorality—unless, that is, we have imbued wealth and poverty themselves with moral weight. None of this deals with the additional reality of a corrupted criminal justice system, the opportunities for wealth to cover up crimes, and the racialized power dynamics at play.[6] And yet each of those realities is deeply impacted by the prosperity gospel: judges, politicians, and lawyers are all influenced by the pervasive belief that financial success is in some way related to moral purity or goodness.

Chris Lehmann, author of *The Money Cult: Capitalism, Christianity, and the Unmaking of the American Dream*, uses the phrase "the Money Cult" to describe the "frank celebration of wealth as a spiritual virtue in American Protestantism."[7] While Lehmann is often discussing the traditional prosperity gospel, he also argues that this characteristic of American Protestantism is near universal. While the story many conservatives would tell is one where America was founded on "Judeo-Christian values" and religious freedom, Lehmann argues that instead of privatizing religion, the American legacy is a deified market.[8] You can worship whoever you want in the privacy of your own home, but in public you worship the all-knowing, perfectly just, all-powerful market.

This gospel is not merely learned; it is the air we breathe. We celebrate each other's financial successes with language that betrays just how much we believe in the prosperity gospel: "You earned this!" "God is blessing your family so much right now." "God is rewarding you." It's a comforting story in the same way a children's bedtime story about princesses and dragons is comforting to a child afraid of the dark: the good guys win, the bad guys lose, and the world is a just place.

Patriotic Gospel

As a military kid, I spent my fair share of time attending military ceremonies, living on military bases, and worshiping in military base chapels.[9] These chapels are strange spaces, where our citizenships—earthly and heavenly—come crashing together. A few years ago, attending a chapel service while visiting my parents, a chaplain said this in the middle of a prayer: "Lord, we know that our service to our country and our service to you do not contradict or conflict." The chaplain may have intended to draw attention to that weekend's observance of Memorial Day, but his statement is dangerously ingrained into American Christian consciousness. While I have not served my country in quite the same way the chaplain was referencing—I may have experienced unique difficulties as a military kid, but I haven't made the sacrifices my dad or others have—even I can recognize places where my service to my country and my service to God conflicted.

This is the second gospel that so deeply affects American Christians: the patriotic gospel. Rather than expressing gratitude for the good gifts given to a particular nation and understanding the special connection members of the same nation share, the patriotic gospel requires uncritical allegiance to one's country. For Christians, it usually takes the form of applying biblical promises or blessings intended for Israel or the church to America. We equate the founding of our country with the creation of a godly nation, our particular political structure as God-ordained, and our leaders as spiritual guides.

Like all of our false gospels, the patriotic gospel slowly but persistently immerses us in a salvific story. We learn that the fundamental problem with the world is that "they" are not like "us." We learn that the solution to feelings of insecurity, threats of discomfort, and the instability of the world is the innate goodness of our country. For Americans, this gospel is imbued with historical beliefs about our status as a nation chosen by God, the faith of our Founding Fathers, and biblical promises we've appropriated for America.

The patriotic gospel thrives on a captivating narrative about a superior nation, her special people, and her mission in the world. It is also a salvific story communicated in symbols, rituals, and sacrifices. The military ceremonies I grew up attending are an obvious example. But everyone grows up with this story: not only do we sing the national anthem at sporting events, state fairs, or military events, but we also practice an established ritual—placing our hands on our hearts as a sign of allegiance. We have national symbols such as the eagle, the Statue of Liberty, and the American flag that make their way onto clothing, décor—anything really. We have a special language for adherents—"America first," "the home of the brave," "the American Dream"—and we sacralize the work of the nation: soldiers have a "sacred" duty, we allude to biblical victories in political discourse, and we sing songs like "God Bless America." We have the Fourth of July, a holiday (holy day) with feasts, displays of these symbols of patriotism, and ritual explosives. Most American children in the last sixty or seventy years have started their school days with the Pledge of Allegiance, a practice so normalized we hardly think about how strange it is for elementary school children to have a pledge of *allegiance* to their country as part of their education. It wasn't until 1945 that the United States had an official Pledge of Allegiance and not until 1954 that the pledge included the phrase "under God"—the result of political and social pressure heightened by a desire to unify the country against the Soviet Union.[10] And yet this fairly recent Pledge of Allegiance and its politically motivated amendment seem to many Americans a crucial aspect of our civic participation and a normal part of the education of every child—that's the power of the patriotic gospel.

The Pledge of Allegiance is one example of many given by those who propagate a particularly Christian version of the patriotic gospel—the idea of this country as a "Christian nation." If America was founded on Christian principles, fueled by Christian values, and specially chosen by God, a critical or prophetic position toward America is increasingly difficult. The pledge is one example of ways that many patriotic references to God became part of our national consciousness much later than the myth of Christian America would have us believe. Debates over the faith of the Founding Fathers, the religious nature of their founding principles, and the meaning of "religious freedom" at the time are complex. Yet even in the midst of a defense of the largely Christian nature of America's founding, which he calls the "weak view of Christian

America," historian Mark Noll argues, "If we really believed the notion of a special manifestation of divine benevolence to America, we would end with a twisted view of God."[11]

When we baptize the history of a nation—America or any other—we put God's character to the test against the history and principles of an earthly nation, instead of the other way around. Placing great emphasis on the founding of America as a site of particular Christian motivation is especially dangerous when you consider that early American history was also marked by the genocide of native peoples, the subjugation of women, and the enslavement of Africans. American Christians, regardless of motives, put a lot at risk when we paint our nation as uniquely Christian—namely, our witness to a world looking at our nation's history without our rose-colored glasses.

If we think that our service and love to our country and to God and his people are completely compatible, we have confused the two or melded them completely. Professor and author David Dark puts it this way: "Does the biblical witness disturb the mental furniture of the average American?"[12] Because if it doesn't, we've accepted the patriotic gospel at the expense of the biblical one. As Dark points out, "When we pray, 'Deliver us from evil,' are we thinking mostly of other people from other countries?"[13] When we think of sin, do we think of that which conflicts with American values? When we think of salvation, do we think of American victory? Few of us would admit to consciously holding these beliefs. And yet many American churches preach a new heaven and new earth that look a lot like cosmic victims of America's myth of Manifest Destiny, or a kingdom of God that is little more than a baptized America.

Like all gospels, the patriotic gospel thrives in our hearts to the extent to which we think it is just the way things are and not unique values and beliefs we have been immersed in for so long that we no longer recognize them. Everyone on earth is formed by the nations and communities they live in—we are finite, contingent beings who rely on other people (usually, the people closest to us) to help us understand and navigate the world. Yet Christians should be the kind of people who can love their nation for its good gifts given by God and also critically engage with its sinful legacy.

The Security Gospel

In a time in our history when our access to information about international instability and disaster is greater than ever before, more Americans mistakenly think crime is rising,[14] and news coverage is 24-7, we also have great interest in crime stories. There are true-crime podcasts, TV shows, documentaries, and entire online communities invested in following crimes. In a world that *feels* less safe than ever before, many of us have a strange fascination in hearing these stories.

The reasons for this are complex, but one explanation might be the strange sense of control true-crime stories give us. I recently listened to a podcast episode about a woman unjustly imprisoned after being assaulted at a bar.[15] Without initially realizing I was doing it, I repeatedly thought to myself, "I wouldn't let that happen to me." I found myself isolating the details in the story where I could find some supposed fault of the woman's and reminding myself that I would never do or say the things she did. I thought if I could put at least some blame on this woman for the crimes against her, I could feel safe.

In reality, there is no foolproof guard against danger and insecurity. People get in car accidents on roads they've driven a hundred times. Diseases infect healthy people. Bombings and shootings happen in places we thought were safe. Our justice system arrests, imprisons, and convicts innocent people.

The world is not a safe place, yet the security gospel promises that we can ensure our own safety, telling us to believe, I can make myself safe. My community can make itself safe. My nation can make itself safe. The world is just and fair, and if I do and say the right things, I will stay safe. Tragedy only happens to people who let it happen. In other words, "You were asking for it."

Very few of us would make any of these beliefs explicit. When I realized what I was thinking about the woman who was assaulted in the bar, I immediately knew I was wrong. Of course none of it was her fault. But as I heard the story, my fear that I could face the same danger was assuaged by my subconscious belief that things like that only happen to people who make bad choices. If the "sin problem" in this gospel is insecurity, then the salvific solution is to protect yourself.

The Christian version of the security gospel focuses on Bible stories where God protects the righteous: freeing Peter from jail, protecting Daniel in the lions' den, parting the waters to get Israel safely across the Red Sea. In the Christian version of the security gospel, God always provides physical security. This version conveniently leaves out the parts of the biblical witness where God allows his people to suffer insecurity or even asks them to do dangerous things: John the Baptist is beheaded for his faithful witness, Paul is jailed and persecuted for following Jesus' command to share the gospel, and Jeremiah is thrown in a pit and left to die because he tells the truth about God's judgment. Paul even describes suffering and insecurity as a normal experience for believers that God can use for their ultimate good (2 Timothy 3:12; 1 Peter 4:12-19; Philippians 1:29).

South African theologian and antiapartheid activist Rev. Dr. Allan A. Boesak said, "When we go before Him, God will ask, 'Where are your wounds?' And we will say, 'I have no wounds.' And God will ask, 'Was there nothing worth fighting for?'"[16] In a broken world, the work of the kingdom of God will require suffering, and our unwillingness to be exposed to danger keeps us from this righteous work. For John the Baptist, Paul, and many of the prophets, faithfulness to God's commands put them in more danger, not less. Their safety and security were secondary (if that) to their desire to faithfully witness to the kingdom of God. While we might like to isolate this reality to those who share the gospel in hostile areas, the prophet was usually speaking God's truth to his own people. Jeremiah is thrown in a pit not just because he tells the people to stop worshiping idols but because the false prophets want to continue telling God's people that they can keep accumulating wealth and exploiting the vulnerable without consequences. They can mistreat the foreigner, the widow, and the orphan, and as long as they come to the temple and do their religious duties every once in a while, they will be fine. They are safe.

Legal scholar Lucia Zedner argues that our desire for security often paradoxically requires a constant reminder of danger. We end up "scattering our social world with visible reminders of the threat of crime"[17] in a way that exacerbates social divisions.[18] Those with financial resources can live in gated communities, avoid "dangerous" neighborhoods and public transportation, or even hire private security. This is one of the consequences of the security gospel: we must prioritize our own safety over meeting the needs of other people. We see this logic in our discomfort interacting with the poor in our own cities, our unwillingness to live and work in impoverished communities, and in fear-based immigration and refugee policies.

Audrey Assad is an award-winning musician, talented songwriter, and the daughter of a Syrian refugee. When asked what she would say to Americans fearful of letting in Muslim refugees, Assad said, "National security is not a kingdom value, but hospitality is."[19] Security is an ultimate, eternal reality for believers in Christ, but earthly bodily security is not guaranteed. Hospitality, laying down our lives for each other, and caring for our neighbors even when it costs us—those are kingdom values.

National security is one example of a macro version of the security gospel, as is our system of mass incarceration. These macro versions have large-scale effects but are also communally believed and practiced. They are propagated in our educational and political institutions, formed and practiced in our communities, and involve structural power and communal meaning making. We may not accept the belief that God grants us individual security, but many of us have accepted the corporate version of this gospel—that the greatest good for our communities and nation is our security, a security that should be fought for at all costs.

For example, the so-called War on Drugs was based in a desire for security that prioritized law and order over restoring and building up communities. Ending drug trafficking and decreasing drug use is a worthy goal, but when it is rooted in fear it produces a deadly system. One illustration of the way fear perverted this desire is in racist enforcement of drug laws. Federal laws, for example, punished crack offenses one hundred times more harshly than powder cocaine offenses—and the majority of people charged with crimes involving crack were black, whereas the majority of people charged with crimes involving powder cocaine were white.[20] When Judge Clyde Cahill was assigned to the case of Edward Clary, an eighteen-year-old convicted under these laws, he argued that even in the absence of explicit racial bias, "fear coupled with unconscious racism had led to a lynch-mob mentality and a desire to control crime—and those deemed responsible for it—at any cost." Cahill argued that fear—of drugs and of the young black men that our national consciousness associates with drug use—was "reinforced by media imagery" and had made a fair legal process close to impossible.[21]

Michelle Alexander writes about these inequalities in her groundbreaking work, *The New Jim Crow*, describing the various ways that legal discrimination morphed into new forms throughout American history—from slavery to sharecropping and Jim Crow to mass incarceration. Alexander details how fear of crime became a strong political motivator in America, from Nixon declaring the "war" in 1971 to Reagan's introduction of federal involvement in 1984. What had historically been the purview of local law enforcement became the concern of the federal government, with massive financial resources allocated to the Federal Bureau of Investigation and Department of Defense. This was the security gospel at work: we believed that with enough resources and harsh enough sentences, we could make our country safe.

In *Strong and Weak: Embracing a Life of Love, Risk and True Flourishing*, Andy Crouch describes how all humans were designed to live with both authority, which he calls "the capacity for meaningful action,"[22] and vulnerability, the "exposure to meaningful risk."[23]

Humans were given authority to rule and steward creation, but we were also created with vulnerability as limited, contingent creatures. God intended us to experience both dimensions of human experience, but the security gospel has no room for vulnerability. As Crouch explains, when humans try to rid themselves of vulnerability, they inevitably offload it on someone else and take authority that doesn't belong to them. Crouch gives the striking example of a local police force: it is an institution intended to produce flourishing for a community, but when it seeks authority without vulnerability, it must take authority from the community and offload its vulnerability onto the people it is supposed to serve.[24] In contrast with community policing, in which relationship building and local engagement are emphasized and both the community and the police have a mix of authority and vulnerability, militarized policing puts all authority in the police and makes the community entirely vulnerable.

Our overriding desire for security can justify anything, including the abuse and degradation of human beings. Whether it's the micro version keeping me from reaching out to the vulnerable or the macro version justifying national policies that keep the rich and powerful safe at the expense of the poor and weak, the security gospel has deeply political implications. It tells us who deserves protection and who must pay for it, it justifies harmful drug and crime policies, and it teaches us who to fear and who to protect. In the security gospel, our sin problem of vulnerability is solved by physical force, harsh policies, and high walls. Protection is the ultimate good, and anything else can be sacrificed at its altar.

The Gospel of White Supremacy

There is one gospel that is simultaneously pervasive in the white American church and most firmly denied by it: the gospel of white supremacy. As we noted earlier, the current iteration of American evangelical political engagement is highly rooted in defending segregation in traditionally white environments of all kinds, and this history is far-reaching. As Jemar Tisby outlines in his historical survey of racism in the American church, *The Color of Compromise*, American Protestants have "written some of the most well-known narratives of racism in the United States."[25] Religious and racial prejudice have been combined since the beginning of our country's history to construct the social category of race, with most American denominations either being formed with provisions for slaveholding members or split over the issue. Scripture was used as a weapon to defend the institution of slavery during the Civil War, and Christians used theological excuses for complicity with Jim Crow laws and opposition to the civil rights movement.

For American Christians in particular, we live in a legacy of white supremacy whether we chose it or not. Our church traditions and practices have been cultivated in a context of white supremacy: for many of us, the most segregated places we regularly visit are our church buildings. We are not merely spiritually formed by ideas but by practices, habits—and places. When the locus of our spiritual formation happens in places deeply influenced by decades of segregation—both cultural and legal—we will likewise be affected.

The sins of the parents will affect the children: it's a remarkably biblical idea that thoroughly permeates the judgments of the prophets. We tend to read that in an individual way about the influence parents have over their children, but the Old Testament rarely focuses on only the nuclear family. A community, a country, a people—they are affected by the sins of previous generations, not only suffering for them but repeating them. In America, our religious imaginations are corrupted by a legacy of slavery and racism, and we will continue to be formed by the gospel of white supremacy until we truly learn our history, wrestle with it, repent of it, and find contextual ways of rectifying it.

We do not have to harbor consciously racist thoughts in order to be impacted by the legacy of our country and religious communities. We live in physical spaces defined by long histories of racist housing and education policies, many still suffer the generational effects of slavery and Jim Crow discrimination, and white Americans still benefit from historical hoarding of power and resources. Even more so than the other gospels—likely because it's less socially acceptable—the gospel of white supremacy thrives on going unnoticed. We probably don't consciously believe that the "sin problem" is people of color, or that the salvific solution is white dominance, but it's a flawed logic we've been immersed in.

It is important that we understand how deep this logic has been ingrained in our national consciousness, often perverting historic Christian practices. In his book *Redeeming Mulatto: A Theology of Race and Christian Hybridity*, Brian Bantum records an antebellum baptismal rite for slaves. It begins, "You declare in the Presence of God and before this Congregation that you do not ask for the holy baptism out of any design to free yourself from the Duty and Obedience you owe to your Master while you live, but merely for the good of Your Soul."[26] Racist logic and language are an integral part of the religious experience, sustaining a certain economy and social structure over and against the Christian gospel. As Bantum explains, "Even the explicitly religious has been co-opted by a reality that is understood to be prior and primary."[27]

As Bantum points out, racist logic is the product of a perverse discipleship. "That racial performance exists as a social phenomenon is certainly a challenge to Christian discipleship. But to suggest it is a religiously grounded form of being in the world is to infer a theological response that must be more precise in its description of the problem and the way forward."[28] When we ignore the ways that racism operates as a form of discipleship, we will fail to properly define it and defeat it. Many of us think of racism as intentionally bigoted beliefs or actions, prejudice against someone that is cognitively affirmed and acted upon. In reality, racism is a system of oppression based in race—a system that is communicated affectively and experientially.[29]

As Beverly Daniel Tatum describes, this communication begins early: most Americans grow up in highly segregated neighborhoods where their experience of people who are different from them is limited to secondhand representations. White Americans in particular grow up in the most isolated social contexts, limiting their interactions and nurturing stereotypes. For people of color, this segregation decreases exposure to the benefits of white communities, such as high rates of civic engagement, influence from educational institutions, and social networks that provide jobs—regardless of socioeconomic status. Some of our earliest social contexts encourage racial stereotyping and inhibit cross-group interactions.[30] Over time, Tatum says, white people passively absorb racial messages of superiority—messages that can go unchallenged for an entire lifetime.[31]

Our discipleship toward racial fidelity starts when we grow up in segregated communities, continues when we consume media that only depicts people who look like us (and often depicts those who don't as dangerous or evil), and solidifies as we combine our implicit biases with particular political positions that further marginalize people of color. This reality cannot be regarded as merely sinful beliefs or actions but as an entire way of life and being in the world, something much harder to resist. The white supremacist gospel tells us that "our kind of people" deserve better, safer, happier lives. The sin problem in the world is the existence of dangerous and different people and anyone who disrupts our blissful ignorance of structural biases and inequalities. In our supposedly postracial society, this gospel must fly under the radar, but that doesn't mean it has ceased to exist.

Michael Emerson and Christian Smith begin their sociological examination of racism among white evangelicals by noting that it is a story of how "well-intentioned people, their values, and their institutions actually recreate racial divisions and inequalities they ostensibly oppose."[32] They powerfully illustrate how evangelicals and their institutions have furthered racial division and hatred throughout America's history, but they remain convinced that one of the central problems is the ignorance that prevents us from seeing our own complicity. Well-meaning white Christians who have been immersed in this white supremacy gospel struggle to grapple with systemic problems because of their commitment to individualism, and they further segregation by their insistence on remaining in racially homogenous religious groups.

Emerson and Smith note that Christian faith has often been the impetus for fighting inequality and seeking justice, but they give a sobering caution to American evangelicals: your desire for racial reconciliation is not enough. Our entanglement within a powerful gospel of white supremacy requires an even more powerful form of counterdiscipleship.

Political Gospels

These gospels are powerful because of their captivating narratives, their comforting beliefs, and the rituals and practices that form them in our lives. While each gospel has its individual characteristics, each is also communal and cultural—making it so powerful because it is part of the societal atmosphere so natural to us that we don't even notice it is there. None of these gospels are handed to us as fully formed "religious" options that we cognitively accept or reject but are experienced more as stories we live into. When Christians contemplate our political engagement, we typically evaluate the beliefs we have accepted or the worldview we are operating out of, but we may be ignorant of these gospels that have infiltrated not just our thinking but also our loving and living. The truly good news, however, is that the Christian gospel is a powerful communal story as well. We already have the resources we need—a cosmic redemptive story, rehearsed in the context of community, through historic language and practices.

FOR THE **Life** OF THE **World**

SPIRITUAL FORMATION AND PUBLIC LIFE

An other-worldly piety, which wants God without his kingdom
and the blessedness of the new soul without the new earth, is really
just as atheistic as the this-worldliness which wants its kingdom without God,
and the earth without the horizon of salvation. God without the world
and the world without God, faith without hope and hope without
faith are merely a mutual corroboration of one another.

JÜRGEN MOLTMANN

What is our salvation for? If you were to ask this question to kids in Sunday school classrooms across the country, you'd probably get a lot of the same answers: "So we go to heaven when we die." "So Jesus comes into our hearts." "So our sins are forgiven." The grown-up Sunday school classes would probably give similar answers. Our salvation is for *us*. We are saved by Jesus' death and resurrection for the purpose of our personal reconciliation with God. Similarly, our *sanctification* is for ourselves: God wants to make us better people—morally upright, spiritually fulfilled, and personally pious.

I do not remember a time where I was not worried about having a daily "quiet time," because I had been taught that Christians are supposed to spend time alone with God every day, praying and reading our Bibles. Most of the messages associated with this practice were about my inner transformation: praying calms you, reading your Bible teaches you, the quiet centers you. You start your day with your quiet time so that you will be a better person throughout the rest of the day.

But what if neither our salvation nor our sanctification are for us? What if the whole story isn't primarily about us and our personal growth? What if God's redemptive plan is the reconciliation of the whole world, and our personal salvation is one part of a larger sweep of redemption? And if that's all true, what would our salvation look like?

While many of us can recognize that our salvation is not just about us, we don't always think of our sanctification or the place it happens—the church—as being *for* other people rather than just with them. We certainly don't think of either our sanctification or the church as oriented toward political issues. That would defy our carefully delineated lines between our public and private lives. The first hurdle to faithful political participation is our focus on personal piety and individual transformation. Perhaps a better way to approach the contentious conversation around politics and faith is to start our conversation here: What are our salvation, our sanctification, and the life of the church *for*?

For the Life of the World

We may conclude that the Christian response to the various gospels vying for our devotion is to isolate ourselves from the world that produces them. Even if we do not literally move out into the wilderness to create a community separated from the rest of the world, we might think the right response to these gospels is to cultivate an isolated subculture, barricading ourselves from worldly influences and developing personal spiritual disciplines that draw our attention further inward. We might not retreat to a commune but into ourselves, seeking insulation from the reach of these gospels. But the problem with this approach is that our spiritual disciplines were never meant to be only about us.

It is certainly true that what we are calling spiritual formation—our spiritual disciplines, our corporate worship, the communities we are formed in—should internally change us. In the first chapter of Colossians, Paul prays for the church to grow in its knowledge of God's will, to gain understanding and live worthy lives, and to be strengthened by God. The fifth chapter of Hebrews uses the illustration of milk and solid food to describe how believers should be growing in their understanding and their ability to distinguish good from evil. Our hearts are changed by our spiritual formation, and we are made into people who imitate Christ more fully and consistently.

In a world focused on perfecting our outward appearances and public personas, a Christian call to cultivating godly character and spiritual growth is necessary and countercultural. For some people, and in certain seasons, concentrated focus on personal growth is appropriate. Especially for those of us experiencing or healing from trauma, walking through suffering, or repenting from destructive sin in our lives, sustained attention to the inner spiritual life is necessary. But as pastor and seminary professor Barry Jones puts it, "When these emphases are elevated to the place of prominence that they sometimes receive, the result can be a truncated vision of Christian spirituality, one that is more concerned with getting us out of the world and the world out of us rather than leading us into the world for the sake of the world."[1]

Our spiritual formation is not merely or even primarily about our personal piety. A focus on "me and Jesus" against the world is an incredibly privileged position.[2] God's redemptive plan throughout history has consistently concerned all of creation, and he repeatedly admonishes his people to seek the flourishing of the whole world. Much of our Old Testament theology is focused on the Mosaic and Davidic covenants and their foundational character for the creation of God's covenant community, Israel. Yet the Noahic covenant (found in Genesis 9) is often ignored: the covenant that God made with all living creatures, the covenant that pulls the entire creation into his redemptive plan. Old Testament scholar Aaron Chalmers argues that the name itself is not representative of the true significance of the covenant, writing that "God's covenant with creation" would be better.[3]

Even God's chosen people, Israel, were commissioned as a light (Isaiah 49:6) and a blessing (Genesis 22:18) to the nations. Their obedience to God's commands, their unique life as a community, and their worship would be a witness to the rest of the world, testifying to the character of Yahweh. Even in captivity, God's people are instructed to seek the peace and prosperity of their captor's city, building homes, planting gardens, and making families (Jeremiah 29:4-7). Their shared life together is a witness to the character of the God who has directed and shaped every aspect of their community—economically, politically, and socially.

Israel's relationship to God was political, formed by a treaty, a covenant. Their vocabulary and self-identify were as a political community organized around law that reflected the character of their ruler and determined their way of life. That God chose to use a nation at the beginning of his redemptive plan for all creation is not an accident.[4] Instead, this community represented a way of life that internally and externally formed them; through the rhythms and rituals of their life together, they were individually made into different people and together made into a different community. Their community was a reflection to the rest of the world of who God is and how he operates.

Walter Brueggemann notes that the very choosing of Israel as God's covenant people is a "scandal of particularity,"[5] whereby God enters into the historical, social, and political reality of a particular people and chooses them as the community through which he will redeem the whole world. They are given commands that shape them into the kind of community that witnesses to this redemptive work. So their existence and regulation as a community does not make much sense if the goal is their own personal righteousness, for they are not only a light to the nations, but their regulation as individuals is constantly tied to the health and righteousness of their entire community. Contrary to our popular conception, then, Old Testament law isn't there to provide a list of rules that no longer apply to us (and thus don't deserve any of our attention), it introduces us to a community whose life together witnessed to God's redemptive plan—both to those inside the community and those outside of it.

Similarly, the early Christians not only brought a message—a propositional truth—that challenged Greco-Roman life and practices, but their community also embodied this challenge. The new reality that Christ had risen was the force that drove the mission, but that mission was "carried to the world by a people whose pattern of communal life is in the very form of the good news."[6] The gospel is universal, but it has been carried by particular people in particular places in the particular (and peculiar) ways they live together.

But believers have also been shaped throughout history by the friction that results from two communities—the earthly nations and cities they inhabit and the global and historic church they belong to—bumping against one another. In AD 112, Pliny the Younger wrote a letter to Trajan, the Roman emperor, in search of advice for dealing with Christians. He described the early church as an "economic nuisance" as it had triggered a loss of revenue for the temples that sold sacrificial animals and other merchandise. He called them a "political club" that took care of the sick, organized community events, buried the impoverished dead, and supported widows and orphans.

Instead of offering what other institutions and communities could offer, the church required and provided a distinctly different social and political ethic that contradicted the surrounding culture. *The Epistle to Diognetus*, an early Christian apologetic, goes back and forth in describing the seemingly contradictory existence of Christians in the world: they dwell in Greek cities, they eat and dress like everyone else, and yet their citizenship "confessedly contradicts expectation." They marry and have children but do not discard unwanted infants. They share meals but not wives. They obey the laws, and yet they surpass them in their goodness. And they have a unique political and social position: "As citizens, they share in all things with others, and yet endure all things as foreigners."[7]

The church was also strange and concerning because of the way it welcomed the most vulnerable and marginalized in society. The apologist Tatian noted that the church included everyone in worship and organization, making "no distinctions in rank and outward appearance, or wealth and education, or age and sex."[8] In a society where Roman men often pressured women to get dangerous abortions and let female infants die of exposure, the Christian community created lower mortality rates for women because of a different social ethic that valued the contributions of women—single and married—for the good of the community. Athenagoras, in the late second century, said of the church, "Among us you will find uneducated persons, artisans, and old women. They may be unable in words to prove the benefit of our doctrine. However, by their deeds, they demonstrate the benefit arising from their accepting its truth."[9]

The church could not create this ethic—of valuing the vulnerable, providing community and accountability for believers, and caring for the sick and poor—by detailing a set of doctrines that required this behavior. Neither was this community formed by practicing inward-focused spiritual disciplines. The communal habits and practices of the early church nurtured and sustained its life in the world—and when the focus of the church was a life lived for the world, personal piety was subsumed under, but not eliminated from, the life of the community. Conversely, when it comes to spiritual disciplines, "quiet time," or church worship, our modern tendency is to prioritize our personal experience—what satisfies, excites, or pleases us. But as professor and author Kyle David Bennett explains, the Christian life "does not involve endless private, mystical experiences that tickle our fancy. Rather, it is the transformation of mundane activities that have vast public implications for our neighbor."[10]

A Political World

Even if our salvation is for the sake of the world—the people of God as a witness to his redemptive work, a sign of his coming kingdom, and a force for flourishing—why does it require political involvement? American Christians have a long legacy of trying to parse out exactly what counts as political so that we can engage with the parts of the world that go untouched by the corrupting influences of politics. But politics color all aspects of our collective life. Disengaging from politics is impossible, and the effort to do so is an abdication of our responsibility as image bearers.

One hurdle to a proper understanding of the relationship between spiritual formation and political engagement is establishing the legitimacy of human government in general. Various theological and historical forces have frequently diminished the significance of human government, either regarding it as entirely evil or as belonging to a lower order of creation. But just as God created humans for cultural and social life, he created them for political life as well. The meaning of that word *political* is important. It can signify *statecraft*—the exercise of coercive power for the sake of ordered governance. However, it also has a broader meaning. It signifies the means by which we shape our common life together. While the creational nature of statecraft has been debated by theologians since the patristic era, there's no real disputing that humans are social creatures and that our common life together is an important theological concern. In this chapter, politics will be used in this wider sense to refer to the various ways humans live together, exercise authority, and seek the common good.

The first commands given to humanity in Genesis 1:28 are to "Be fruitful and increase in number; fill the earth and subdue it. Rule over the fish in the sea and the birds in the sky and over every living creature that moves on the ground." Political action begins in creation, as Adam and Eve are given instructions to discover and creatively use the natural resources God has gifted them. They are commissioned to cultivate his creation, to be agents of his rule on earth, and to create further order and beauty within it. The image is a way of "authorizing" humanity—delegating the legitimate exercise of power and use of resources in order to further God's purpose on earth. This concept of the *imago Dei* is rooted in the Ancient Near Eastern concept of the "image of God" bestowed on kings as earthly representatives of divine rule.[11] The inextricable linking of the *imago Dei* with the delegation of authority means that unlike the Babylonian and Assyrian empires that concentrated power in a few privileged people, the Genesis account dignifies political work as the shared task of humanity.[12]

I've written much of this book in coffee shops—wonderful examples of humanity's creative authority in the world. It starts when a person takes a part of God's good creation, coffee beans, and cultivates them, harvests them, and to this natural resource applies creativity—roasting, grinding, brewing—and makes something new and beautiful out of it. Then some other people decide they want to sell the fruit of their labors to others, but instead of offering a merely transactional experience, they decide to create something new: a space where people can enjoy the cultural artifact they have created, in community. They apply their human creative capacities to build an aesthetically pleasing shop, design a menu, and promote their vision for their business. Then people come and build their own creative projects in the coffee shop—relationships, businesses, music, writing, art. The place fosters community and creativity of its own.

Politics reflects our good creational order in the same way—humans take the raw materials God has blessed his creation with—such as intelligence, land, and human relationships—and they creatively cultivate those things. Some of our other pursuits require the creative endeavor of politics to function well: our businesses need roads and city plans, the conflicting interests of our enterprises need mediation, our societies need guardrails for creative production. And just as a coffee shop can exploit its workers, shortchange its customers, or merely prioritize moneymaking over community making, our political systems and political work are impacted by our sinful nature and broken world. That fact does not make those creative endeavors irredeemable or ultimately worthless; it makes them imperfect witnesses to God's good creation, just as everything else we do.

The very makeup of Israel as a community is evidence that God is not indifferent about material communal realities like patterns of land use and ownership, family obligations, and our stewardship of economic resources. The institution of sabbath, which we often associate with spiritual renewal or physical rest, was more fundamentally an institution through which to regulate economic and social life around God's provision for the poor and wealthy alike. We tend to disregard the particular legal regulations that formed Israel as a nation, but they illuminate an important theological truth: God cares about the ordinary and procedural ways that we organize our communities.

Our participation in politics, then, is an expression of the created order and our created identity, and it is revelatory of the fulfillment of God's creative redemption. The picture in Revelation of the ultimate reconciliation of humanity and God, the perfect redemption of heaven and earth, is not the same as the picture in the beginning. Redemption doesn't mean everything goes back to its original condition. Instead of returning to the garden, eternal redemption comes to us in the imagery of a city. Revelation 21 describes a new Jerusalem, a well-ordered city that represents human flourishing and creativity in all its fullness: perfect relationship with our Creator, perfect freedom to work for the common good, and the perfectly governed human community. While the church is our foundational human community and authority on earth, the new heaven and new earth don't have a place of worship because God dwells with his people. The redeemed earth will not have a church, but it will have a city. Our vocation to steward God's creation does not end, but finds its redeemed expression in our work in a city.

Ironically, the passages most often referenced in support of political disengagement—such as Philippians 3:20, Hebrews 13:14, and Ephesians 2:19—tell us that our citizenship is in heaven, meaning that one element of our eternal identity is political affiliation with the coming kingdom of God. Instead of viewing this life, including our political participation during it, as simply biding our time until our true citizenship is fully realized, we should view our engagement in this age as a glimpse and a foretaste of that future. The work that we do now will be redeemed, not extinguished. Our current engagements anticipate our future engagements, transcending the limitations of earthly political work and providing opportunities for us to witness to a larger project of human flourishing. Our work in the here and now is nurturing our political imaginations for the life to come.

Jesus' life and ministry took place in a particularly politically charged environment—the Jewish people were living under the rule of a foreign power, and different religious groups held different opinions about the right political posture to take in response. Everything Jesus said and did would be interpreted and reinterpreted in light of discerning what kind of political future you believed God promised your people.

It is in this context that Jesus preached the coming *kingdom* of God, accepted political enemies like zealots and tax collectors together into one community, and consistently denied the ultimate authority of Rome. According to Luke, the last question asked of Jesus is found in Acts 1:6: "Lord, are you at this time going to restore the kingdom to Israel?" Many interpret this exchange as one last time where the disciples completely misunderstand Jesus. They are awaiting a physical kingdom, and they still have not figured out that he has come to bring a spiritual one. But Jesus doesn't tell them the question itself is wrong. Instead, he tells them that it is not for them to know the time of his return (v. 7) and that they have a job to do in the meantime (v. 8). While the disciples are thinking within the realm of Roman-controlled Israel and the promise of their freedom, Jesus is speaking of a worldwide kingdom that encompasses Jews and Gentiles. His Spirit will come upon them and send them outside of Israel, to the "ends of the earth." The point is not that the kingdom is purely spiritual, but that it extends to the entire world. All of this means that when Jesus says that his kingdom is "not of this world" (John 18:36), he's not saying it has nothing to do with this world. His kingdom does not conform to the expectations and paradigms of this world, nor does it follow the rules that earthly rulers do. As Jesus tells his disciples, the earthly authorities hoard and misuse their power, but his kingdom is marked by sacrifice and self-giving love (Matthew 20:25).

Jesus' ministry is not apolitical; it reorients the perspective of his people and refuses to acquiesce to the narrow political categories of his world. When Jesus says to Pilate, "You would have no power over me if it were not given to you from above" (John 19:11), he is not denying Pilate's authority but acknowledging its legitimacy—Pilate's authority is a consequence of legitimate authority delegated by God. While some of Jesus' opponents operate in the context of Rome's power, using imperial methods such as crucifixion to further their goals of getting rid of a religious and political threat to their authority, Jesus' acknowledgment of the legitimacy of human government rightfully situates Pilate's authority as derived from God.

When Jesus says, "Give back to Caesar what is Caesar's and to God what is God's" (Mark 12:17), he is saying, "Give to God what is God's, namely, everything. And under that overall obligation, give what is due to every servant of God—rulers, priests, parents, tax collectors, teachers, prophets, and others."[13] Jesus' answer about taxation also subtly demotes Caesar: instead of his supposed position of divinity, Caesar was another servant of God, one given legitimate—and yet limited—authority.

So instead of viewing the particular institution of human government as God imposing an inherently evil system on his people, our political participation should be viewed as one of many ways we practice the creativity and stewardship we were created for. All work is meant to produce flourishing, and yet all such efforts are distorted by sin. The "powers and principalities" work in and through institutions to subvert their good intentions, yet instead of viewing human government as inherently evil, it is more faithful to the biblical witness to view it as we should all aspects of God's creation—an opportunity to live out our identity as image bearers, with the desire to glorify God and the humble awareness that our efforts will be tainted by sin.[14]

Political Responsibility

Our political participation is both creational and anticipatory. Humans were commanded from the beginning to bear the image of God in our creative work and rule, and our earthly work anticipates the continuation and perfection of this work in eternity. Yet there's an obvious difference: both the created order and its eventual redemption are contexts in which sin does not reign and all humans have relationship with the Creator. The reality today is complicated: as we've noted, political systems are affected by human sin and earthly brokenness, Christians must live and work with nonbelievers, and we have been given commands for this meantime—"Make disciples of all nations" (Matthew 28:19)—that seem to conflict with this political responsibility.

What does Christian political responsibility look like in our fallen world? We can break this big question into three smaller questions: What requirements are given to the noncovenantal nations we live in? How does this responsibility interact with our mission to share the gospel? How can we create flourishing in a sinful world?

1. What requirements are given to the noncovenantal nations we live in? There's a common complaint made both against Christians from non-Christians and between Christians of differing political persuasions— that they need to stop "legislating morality." There are two different implications this accusation can have: that there is a difference between your inner, private morality and your outward political positions—which is false—and that there is a difference between the set of moral rules that Christians are expected to personally uphold and the ones that our non-Christian nation should enforce for the common good of all people— which is true. There is clearly a difference throughout Scripture between the expectations God has for those he has made specific covenants with and those he has not.

The prophets consistently illustrate this difference: they express God's judgment on his people for violating the specific requirements of the covenant—worshiping idols, disobeying his commands, improperly executing his required way of life and worship, for example—but whenever the prophets express his judgment on other nations, there are no prophecies against them for not following instructions and commandments they were never given. Instead, the prophets express God's judgment against other nations when they do not live up to the requirements of the covenant made with all people: the Noahic covenant in Genesis 9. This covenant is made with "all life on the earth" (9:17) and requires that human life be honored and protected, because all human beings are made in the image of God (9:6). So when the prophets express God's judgment on other nations, it is for war-mongering, breaking treaties between nations, selling people into slavery, attacking and mistreating the vulnerable, ruling with arrogance and tyranny, and worshiping false gods (which never works out well for honoring and protecting human life).[15] The prophetic condemnation of Egypt is a striking example: this seemingly all-powerful earthly kingdom is condemned not merely for her wrongs against Israel but for what Old Testament scholar Terence E. Fretheim calls "anti-life measures against God's creation."[16]

Psalm 82 gives a beautiful and succinct picture of how God deals with the whole world. It begins with a statement about God's legitimate power of judgment (v. 1), condemns the nations and their false gods for their unjust legal decisions that favor the wicked (v. 2), exhorts them to defend the vulnerable, oppressed, suffering (v. 3), and the poor (v. 4). It acknowledges that those outside of God's people are both ignorant of his rule (v. 5) and have worthless gods to rule them (v. 7). God's judgment is required, because even for nations following the dictates of their own idols and unaware of God's law (Psalm 147:20), he is ultimately in authority over all of his creation and will legitimately judge against injustice.

None of these scriptural guidelines make it perfectly clear which political questions are issues of distinctively Christian morality and which ones nations will be judged for. In one way or another, almost any political or moral issue is about the honor and protection of human beings. In reality, every piece of legislation is trying to legislate morality. Every policy issue is based on moral principles and has moral implications.

Figuring out how to apply the scriptural principle that God holds all nations and people accountable for the protection and honor of human life in political discussions today is tricky, but it must be attempted.[17]

2. How does this responsibility interact with our mission to share the gospel? If you grew up in Sunday schools anything like the ones I did, it might be a bit jarring to think that we have any responsibility other than the one given in Matthew 28:19, to "go and make disciples of all nations." You may have been taught that our job is to share the gospel, and anything else is either unnecessary or a dangerous distraction from the real mission.

That is, unless your work is both creational and anticipatory—reflective of what it means to be human and a glimpse of human work in a redeemed world. If your salvation, your sanctification, and the church are for the sake of the world—preaching the gospel, seeking the flourishing of the world, and previewing the coming kingdom of God—then there is no conflict between these means of being *for* the life of the world.

All of Scripture has something to say about your life and mission, not just a single verse we have dubbed the "Great Commission," ripped from the life and ministry of the God-man who said it, to be transplanted into any and all cultural contexts. Even the commission itself includes more than we often give it credit for: Jesus tells his disciples to baptize these disciples, teach them everything he has commanded them, and remember that he is with them, to the end of the age (Matthew 28:19-20). He tells them to be the church: to share the gospel by nurturing new believers, initiating them into the community, teaching them, and reminding them he is with them.

The only way that we think a conflict exists between the Great Commission and a church living out its mission for the life of the world is if we've bought into an immaterial, disembodied gospel confined to our personal piety. It'd be like an ambassador from a foreign nation refusing to talk about the social or political makeup of their country and focusing solely on the invitation to become a citizen. Jesus' life and ministry were a witness to God's coming kingdom, and he preached the coming kingdom in sermons and meals, healings and miracles, and while turning over tables and hanging out with little kids.

There are many reasons why American evangelicals are characteristically uncomfortable with prioritizing the social or political aspects of the gospel. But the reality is that this gospel we're so eager to defend comes with an ethic we cannot avoid. There's a reason the prophets spend so much time judging God's people for their social injustice and the epistles spend so much time encouraging hospitality and condemning prejudice and class division among believers. There's a reason that when an expert in religious law tests Jesus about the greatest commandment, Jesus answers, "'Love the Lord your God with all your heart and with all your soul and with all your mind.' This is the first and greatest commandment. And the second is like it: 'Love your neighbor as yourself.' All the Law and the Prophets hang on these two commandments" (Matthew 22:37-40). So the gospel comes with an ethical imperative to love our neighbor, and Scripture is clear that loving our neighbor means opposing social and political barriers to their flourishing.

3. Can we do anything worthwhile in a fallen world? "It's not a skin problem, it's a sin problem." I remember the first time I heard this little phrase in chapel in college. The preacher was willing to acknowledge that racism existed—in explicit, intentional forms only—but felt that making the issue "political" made it impossible to deal with, since the real issue was about sin.

I seriously doubt that this preacher or anyone else who uses this reasoning would apply the same logic to traditional Christian political convictions such as abortion, religious freedom, or gay marriage. I can't imagine such a preacher saying, "It's not an abortion problem, it's a sin problem." Just as we selectively choose what counts as "political" in order to exclude or include it from Christian concern, we selectively choose what issues warrant Christian political engagement and what issues are out of our reach because of sin. Can issues like racism or sexism be legislated away? Of course not. But the reality of sin as a force at work in the world should not lead us to shy away from political engagement.

An approach like this plays best to the politically uninterested. It can be comforting to believe that sin makes our political engagement pointless, because it absolves us of any responsibility and gives convenient theological justification to our apathy. Political uninterest thrives in places of privilege. It could be argued that a considerable number of white American Christians enjoy the necessary privilege to be unaffected by the results of national policy changes or local ordinances. Changes in immigration policy don't affect me as a natural-born citizen, so I have the privilege to ignore it. On a much smaller scale, I live in a comfortable apartment, and trash service comes and picks up the trash in my apartment complex every week, so I have the privilege to ignore local ordinances concerning neighborhoods that don't receive that service. I also have the racial, social, and economic privilege to move to another neighborhood if the city decides to stop providing trash service to my apartment or access to the right resources to fight an unjust policy.

The reality of sin in our world should keep us from placing our ultimate hope in earthly policies or institutions, and it should keep us humble about our own abilities and motives. But it should not keep us from being involved in the political realities that impact our neighbors, even if they don't affect us. I love what author and artist Makoto Fujimura calls "border-stalkers,"[18] people who move in and out of different cultural spheres, institutions, or organizations. He's talking about Christian artists who live in artistic communities and the church, but I think the term could also be applied to Christians who want to nurture their church and local communities. Rather than isolating ourselves away in a Christian subculture, border-stalker Christians sustain themselves in the local church for the sake of faithful stewardship of their neighborhood.

Cultural Estuaries for a Political World

Each of these questions can help us wade through the quagmire that is our political engagement as Christians. But more foundationally than each of them is the reality that Jonathan Leeman puts so succinctly: "The Spirit and the law-implanted heart cannot not enter the ballot box, the jury stand, the legislative chamber, the newspaper editorial office, the protest line or the workplace."[19] As much as we might try (and we do try) to bifurcate our lives along religious and political lines, between our private and public lives and our partisan and moral beliefs—we cannot do it. One story will reign supreme, one kingdom will win our allegiance, one Lord will direct our lives.

Fujimura also uses the language of "cultural estuaries" to describe the places we learn how to do this well. Estuaries are unique ecosystems where salt water and fresh water mix, creating multiple ecological layers and diverse habitats for different creatures. While the broader bodies of water—the river or ocean that feeds into the estuary—are wildly diverse places, they create smaller habitats that prepare different creatures to interact with the wider diversity around them. They are "nurturing—but not isolated—habitats" that strengthen creatures to exist outside of their communities.[20]

There's something to learn there about the church. If political engagement is fraught with strongly formative alternate gospels, kingdoms demanding our allegiance and narratives crawling under our skin, how are we supposed to navigate our responsibility to politically engage? That is what we'll explore in the next few chapters: how the "cultural estuary" of the church is supposed to make it possible for us to swim out into the swirling, diverse world of the wider ocean.

A **Story** TO **Live Into**

SCRIPTURE AND POLITICAL FORMATION

*No task is more important than for the Church to take the
Bible out of the hands of individual Christians in North America. . . .
North American Christians are trained to believe that they are capable of
reading the Bible without spiritual and moral transformation. They read the
Bible not as Christians, not as a people set apart, but as democratic
citizens who think their "common sense" is sufficient
for "understanding" the Scripture.*

STANLEY HAUERWAS

American evangelicals pride themselves on their "high view" of Scripture. Many of us grew up singing the B-I-B-L-E song or competing in "sword drills" to see who could look up a specific verse the quickest. We faithfully tote our impressively thick study Bibles to Sunday morning service to follow along with the sermon. We even put up Bible verses all over our homes, on journals, coffee mugs, and T-shirts.

Evangelicals in particular define ourselves by the prominent place Scripture takes in our theology and lives. Even within the world of conservative Christianity, we divide ourselves up into camps and traditions based on our particular approaches to Scripture. Scripture is full of moral, social, and political instructions for God's people. And while there are deep and legitimate differences of opinion on how to understand and interpret Scripture, many of the barriers to our political formation lie in our inability to recognize our own hermeneutical tendencies, biases, and perspectives. We easily fool ourselves into believing that we're "just reading the text," without interrogating how. One of the most important things we can do for our political formation is to learn to recognize the ways we've been conditioned to read Scripture.

Lesson Learned

As a busy seminary student, I made the smart move one semester to match two of my classes to the Bible study I was leading every week. As I studied the Old Testament prophets for seminary credit, I led our group through the book of Jeremiah. I was taking a Bible class on the Old Testament prophets as well as a Hebrew exegesis class on poetic and prophetic literature. These classes were informative, helpful introductions to the major points of prophetic literature. But perhaps most revealing was the uncomfortable reality that even the most politically conservative professor or student couldn't get around: the prophets have a lot to say about social injustice.

Studying the prophets was like being let in on a secret. Where had this stuff been hiding all my life? I sheepishly told a professor that I couldn't understand how I had read the Bible so much as a kid and still missed the glaring emphasis on injustice, exploitation, and corruption. "Why has no one ever told me about this?" I blurted out, before quickly adding, "I should have seen it." I instantly felt guilt for pushing the blame on others, since I knew it was my own fault that I hadn't been reading the Bible well enough. It wasn't until my Bible study group at church got deeper into Jeremiah that I witnessed from a new perspective just how much of our reading of Scripture is constrained by the political and social influences in our lives.

The first few nights our Bible study went over the beginning chapters of Jeremiah were a little rough. There's a lot of judgment in those first few chapters: for unfaithfulness, idolatry, and injustice. I was worried about explaining and grappling with these difficult texts, but our group was full of women who had grown up in evangelical churches. They didn't flinch at the thought of God harshly judging his people. What they weren't accustomed to, however, was the second question I asked: "What is Israel being judged for?"

"Idolatry!" That was the easy answer. "Unfaithfulness, disloyalty, disobedience." We all knew the big story to fit Jeremiah into: God judges Israel for their disobedience, a lot. But that wasn't the answer I was looking for. "What does disobedience *look like* in these chapters?" I asked. "What were they actually *doing*?" Lots of Bible pages turned, but most of the answers were the same. We had a lens for reading Scripture, and words like *idolatry* and *unfaithfulness* were highlighted in bright yellow. Words like *injustice* and *oppression*, even when they were clearly written in our Bibles, were hot-button political buzzwords to avoid. "What specific sins have they committed?" I asked. "Yes, they have worshiped false gods. What did that look like? What did that cause them to do?"

This is what we learn about disobedience from the first six chapters of Jeremiah: it looks like worshiping empty sources of power (2:5), finding security and comfort in earthly nations and rulers (2:13), harming the ones who call out your sin (2:30), abusing the poor when they have done you no wrong (2:34), denying your own sin (2:35), relying upon political alliances for security (2:36), refusing to change (5:3), growing rich and powerful off the exploitation of the vulnerable and poor (5:27-28), and oppression (6:6).

You cannot read the prophets honestly and walk away thinking God cares more about your personal relationship with him than he does the way you treat other people. Perhaps more urgently for the people of the church, he cares a lot more about how a community treats their most vulnerable—including the flawed social structures that oppress them—than he cares about the religious activities we dutifully perform. Jeremiah is a remarkably relevant book for the American church today, but more than anything else, our little small group's study of the prophet taught me about how easily we can ignore these messages and themes when we aren't conscious and critical of our own blinders.

Getting Good Posture

Many conversations about Christian political engagement are (rightly) based in understanding what Scripture says—about human government, ethical imperatives for believers, and the role of the church in public life. My goal is not to make too many arguments along those lines but to highlight some of the practices and habits that can shift the needle on our political formation from being primarily formed by outside forces to being primarily formed by the Word and by the people of God. The following suggestions for practices or approaches to Scripture are grounded in the belief that we were intended to learn and grow in community. The church is not accidental to Christianity but central; not merely a social opportunity to confirm your prior relationship to God, but the locus of a Christian's life.[1] None of these suggestions make much difference in the life of an individual disconnected from the gift and requirement of a diverse community.

Most of these suggestions are not practices or habits in the truest sense—they are not particular methods or instructions about how to read Scripture. They're more like attitudes or approaches to Scripture that help us recognize our own biases. It's a little bit like learning how to have good posture—you keep adjusting how you sit or stand until it becomes more natural to maintain the right position. Good posture isn't so much about repeating an action over and over again but about consistently checking yourself and adjusting accordingly. Just like my friend's exacerbated comment in chapter one, the question might not be "Are we reading the same Bible?" but "Are we reading it the right way?"

The Necessity of Community

In their fantastic work on church ministry and culture, *Resident Aliens: Life in the Christian Colony*, Stanley Hauerwas and William Willimon argue that both fundamentalists (the "conservatives") and proponents of the historical-critical method (the "liberals") have the same problem with the Bible: they "assume that it is possible to understand the biblical text without training, without moral formation, without the confession and forgiveness that come about within the church."[2] Conservatives who pride themselves on sticking to the Bible and liberals who think that they have all the right tools for proper biblical interpretation are all guilty of the same mistake: we have missed a central implication of our own depravity and put far too much stock in our own ability to understand and apply Scripture by ourselves.

If there's anything I learned in church as a child, it was that the foundation of the Christian life was the "quiet time"—just you and your Bible against the world. After a particularly inspiring youth conference, I set out to read the whole Bible in a year, armed with a study Bible and a thin spiral notebook with "Questions I Have About the Bible" scrawled in Sharpie on the cover. I spent every day that year diligently reading through my Bible and writing pages of questions after each passage. On some days, my quiet time was as inspiring and motivating as I'd been promised, but on other days the questions grew more serious and concerning. I'm thankful for the influences in my life that led a thirteen-year-old to so diligently read Scripture and to feel comfortable enough to write long lists of questions. And yet I now know that I was trying to do the same thing that Hauerwas and Willimon blast Bible scholars for—I thought the Bible was an instruction manual I could follow, without a community to correct my wrong interpretations and train me to apply the right ones to my life.

Scripture itself gives us this clue to its right reading and application. Paul instructs Timothy: "Until I come, devote yourself to the public reading of Scripture, to preaching and to teaching" (1 Timothy 4:13). In his instructions to "watch your life and doctrine closely" (1 Timothy 4:16), Paul includes public reading of Scripture. In Luke 4, Jesus returns to Nazareth after he begins teaching in the synagogues, where he reads aloud from Isaiah, the standard practice for hearing and interpreting Scripture. Likewise, the epistles were instruction and encouragement for the early churches, given by their public reading (Colossians 4:16; 1 Thessalonians 5:27). Communal readings were common in the first few centuries for all kinds of literature and documents, a tradition that the church embraced for Scripture.[3] Tertullian specifically mentions the communal reading of Scripture as definitive of Christian gathering: "We meet to read the books of God."[4] In discussions about canonical and noncanonical books, the instructions are often along the lines of what books should be read privately and those that should be read publicly.[5] The community was constituted by public reading, and so only accepted Scripture should be used in this way.

Public reading remained the primary way for Christians to learn Scripture for much of the history of the church. Until the advent of the printing press, Bibles were so expensive and time-consuming to produce that few individuals could own one. Yet the Bible remained a powerful source of instruction and cultural formation for even the poor and illiterate. In a seeming contradiction, medieval laypeople were both illiterate and biblically knowledgeable. According to historian Lori Anne Ferrell, this is not "such a startling paradox if we enlarge our notion of what might constitute biblical understanding and how it might have been acquired in the age before print and Protestantism."[6] If we assume biblical knowledge comes via personal study and individual application, then most believers had none for a large portion of church history. But if we recognize that Scripture is experienced in communal reading via the moral formation of the ecclesiastical community, then these believers were more "biblically literate" than we are. They heard the Bible read aloud every week of their lives and experienced it at every level of the church gathering—in readings, liturgy, and prayers.

What does any of this have to do with our political formation? The community of God has always been shaped—morally, spiritually, and politically—by gathering together. If we want the truths of Scripture to push back against the strong politically formative forces in our lives, that change will not come about in isolated study that disconnects us from the community of faith. Scripture provides the "paradigm for life within the believing community."[7] That paradigm is best understood as part of the community it is supposed to be forming.

An emphasis on communal reading of Scripture in its various ways also shapes our responsibility to those outside of us—we are not ours alone; we belong to a community that is necessary for our moral formation. The idea that our identity is based in a messy group of people who are not like us is a politically radical idea. When we read Scripture with the needs and burdens of other people in mind, it changes our perspective. This makes it much more difficult to remain neutral on the issues the vulnerable and oppressed face in your own community when you read scriptural commands about caring for them while sitting just a pew away from people in need.

The harsh reality here is that many churches are not the kind of communities we are supposed to be: diverse places where social divisions are abolished. In America, our churches are often the most racially and class-divided places in society. One consequence of spiritualizing the commands of Scripture is that we've lost the ability to see the material and social commands that the New Testament gives the church—to fight prejudice and classism (1 Corinthians 11:18-22), rectify injustices (Acts 6:1-7), oppose racism (Ephesians 2:11-22), and prioritize the needs of the poor (James 2:1-12). It's a vicious cycle: our communities are too homogenous and isolated to read and understand these passages correctly, but properly understanding them is what gives us the impetus to more actively oppose our divisions.

We tend to look around at our churches, see harmony and peace within the relatively homogenous group, and think we're doing all right when it comes to scriptural commands to seek unity and oppose discrimination. What we fail to recognize is that our churches are often the result of fragmentation, not at all the solution to it. We can't pat ourselves on the back for maintaining a unified church if all we're looking at are the people who show up on a Sunday morning. We need to ask who is absent, not necessarily by literal barrier but by social and economic divisions we have failed to properly dismantle in our own community. If our churches are not truly welcoming places for the poor and marginalized, we might not even notice those people being absent. That's not unity—that's discrimination.

There's another way we read Scripture in community: reading with the historic community of the church. One of the reasons many young evangelicals are drawn to more liturgical traditions is because they are hungry for a sense of rootedness. As many of us become more transient—moving across the country for work, living in neighborhoods or apartment complexes with neighbors we don't speak to—there is comfort in tradition and history, in knowing that your theological positions and worship practices are tethered to generations before you. Relying on the rich tradition of the Christian community throughout history helps check some of our contemporary biases; we gain resources from Christians in vastly different social and political contexts from our own.

In one of my seminary classes on spiritual formation throughout church history, the professor was adamant that we approach each new thinker or movement with charity rather than suspicion. During a class discussion about mystical spiritual experiences, a student finally burst out, "But it's just so *weird!*" So in my own desire for charity, I began to imagine what some of these historic figures like Gregory of Nyssa or Julian of Norwich would think of services at evangelical churches today. Our modern skepticism of the supernatural, our focus on teaching over practice, our individualism and consumerism—wouldn't they think we were pretty weird too? In fact, they'd probably be a little taken aback, just like some of my fellow students were when reading some mystics. Reading Scripture with the historic community of faith roots us, but it can also rightly unsettle us. We are newly aware of the places we have capitulated to our current political or economic systems and the cultural sins we've excused, because the places prior generations err are rarely the same as our own.

Karl Barth described the work of dogmatics as starting with "the question of how the Church talked about God yesterday" and asking how it should be done tomorrow.[8] If we are to rightly understand and

apply Scripture, we need to first know what the church has said—both
to be more firmly rooted in our own history and tradition and to have
our eyes opened to the places we have strayed from orthodoxy. Even if
we live in homogenous communities, we can learn from persecuted and
marginalized Christians throughout history and across the globe, such
as the black church in America, persecuted Christians in Asia and
Eastern Europe, and the Confessing Church during the Nazi regime.
Community is the controlling concept for everything else we will say
about Scripture and political engagement. It is the greatest safeguard
we have against misusing Scripture, misunderstanding it, or misap-
plying it—especially when it comes to our own politically influenced
biases and blinders. The global and historic community of the church
provides a diversity of perspectives, experiences, and questions. We all
approach the text with our own prejudices, look to it with our expectations about what it will say, and hear certain ideas louder and clearer
when they speak to our fears or burdens. Therefore, we will only be
challenged and refined by these different perspectives when we treat
the church as the locus of our moral and spiritual formation, the place
that teaches us what the Bible says and how to read it.

Practices for Good Posture

Reading the whole story. Reading Scripture by yourself is one pitfall
to avoid; reading only portions of it is another. Even in churches that
hold a high view of Scripture and pride themselves on their expositional
approach to preaching and teaching, there often remains a significant
blinder: our own selection of what Scripture to read and teach. Many
American evangelical churches follow their own schedule for teaching
and preaching—a handful of sermon series every year and a selection
of Bible studies or classes for each season. We may cover a smattering
of different books every year, hopefully a couple from both the Old and
New Testaments. But the selection is up to someone's discretion—their
appraisal of what the church needs to hear. That's not necessarily a
negative. It recognizes the duty pastors or teachers have to assess what

their people need. Yet the problem with that model remains: we miss exposure to the whole story of Scripture.

James K. A. Smith argues in *Awaiting the King* that the use of a lectionary is a powerful political act because it exposes the community to the whole of Scripture, "including those parts that challenge our own preferences and haunt our learned political leanings."[9] Whether a church uses the lectionary or finds intentional ways to bring the congregation through the whole counsel of Scripture on a regular basis, it is theologically necessary and politically important to confront ourselves regularly with even the most uncomfortable parts of Scripture. The congregations tempted to stick to sexual ethics and end-times judgment will be confronted by widows, orphans, and foreigners; the congregations tempted to stick to widows and orphans will be confronted by countercultural sexual ethics and promises of judgment for evil. "Insofar as hearing the whole counsel of God is a political discipline," Smith writes, "the lectionary is a rite of the kingdom of God."[10]

Whatever the means, the whole story of God's redemptive work on earth should inform and animate the life of the community of faith. And this is not just about preaching or reading Scripture. Historically, Scripture has been woven through all of our communal practices, especially since the sermon has not always had the prominent place it has achieved in American evangelicalism. The communal confession and singing, the Eucharist, and the benediction were soaked in Scripture and thus were the shared language that new believers had to learn, practice, and slowly use for themselves. Yet all church practices are only intelligible as one learns the language of Scripture. We can go through the motions of the habits and practices of our faith community, but if we don't speak the same language, these habits and practices won't have the same effect. Oliver O'Donovan puts it this way: "Liturgical practice can be no better than the lectionary that supports it."[11] That is, if our churches aren't learning the language of Scripture, our practice falls flat.

Our posture toward Scripture means that we don't just read and learn from the whole counsel of Scripture, via a lectionary or otherwise, but that we read it *as a whole story*. Our approach cannot be one that understands Scripture as a set of isolated instructions or moralistic tales plucked from their context. That approach is a recipe for political idolatry, since it leaves plenty of room for cherry-picking and few guardrails for application.

Reading and teaching Scripture as a single redemptive story gives the church a narrative to live into: a story that particularly gives context to our own divisive historical moment. One of the most politically powerful forces in the world might just be a community of people who are not disjointed by the things that fragment the world—that's what Scripture is supposed to protect us from. Without a redemptive story to live into, we're forced to constantly account for new information and adjust our ideologies accordingly.

God's response to the fear of his people living in an insecure, unstable world has always been to tell a story: to remind his people that he brought them out of Israel, that he brought them out of exile, that he raised his son Jesus Christ from the dead.[12] His promises of provision and security, as well as his condemnation of our sin, are backed up by a story about who he is and what he has done for his people in the past. Before his condemnation of idolatry, God gives the basis for this command, a story that displays his character: "I am the LORD your God, who brought you out of Egypt, out of the land of slavery. You shall have no other gods before me" (Deuteronomy 5:6-7).

If we want our response to Scripture to move from interpretation to obedience, it will require our immersion in a community saturated in Scripture's story about who God is. When we rehearse the story of God's provision and protection of his people throughout history, we are better able to obey the command to put our hope and trust in no other "gods," whatever political party they may represent.

Practicing lament. One of the most politically significant ways that the language of Scripture changes us is through the form of lament. We live in a world that is just as divided and troubled as ever but with ever-increasing access to constant news updates, the opinions of fear-mongering pundits, and social media brawls. We're surrounded by people and institutions that want to pump us full of fear and anger for the sake of their own agendas, even if that fear and anger is not necessarily misplaced. The world really is full of injustice and violence, and our response to evil should be righteous indignation. But the outlets we are offered by the world rarely lead to health and restoration.

Scripture offers us a wealth of resources for lamenting and petitioning God for justice and redemption. The greatest portion of the biblical psalms are psalms of lament, many of which are communal laments for communal sins or injustice (Psalms 12, 58, 80, and 83, just to name a few). In *Christian Hospitality and Muslim Immigration in an Age of Fear*, Matthew Kaemingk gives a stunning example of the forms of communal lament people reach for without the guidance of Scripture. In 2011, right-wing nationalists in the Netherlands created a website that allowed citizens to post complaints about their Eastern European immigrant neighbors. While there is a real human need to grapple with the fear and discomfort of a changing world, a platform like this elevates bigotry and violence above reconciliation and proves that "not all spaces of lament are created equal."[13] In a world full of real dangers, differences, and conflict, the answer to prejudice and injustice is neither to elevate nor ignore these dynamics. Scriptural lament has the unique ability to connect to the universal human experience of insecurity and fear without legitimizing the bigotry it can turn into.

The twenty-four-hour news cycle has given many communities more access to information about terrorist attacks, international conflict, and crime than ever before. On one hand, this can be an opportunity to unite communities across geography, create empathy from a distance, or alert churches about issues affecting their brothers and sisters around the world. On the other hand, it can contribute to a culture of fear and suspicion that gives greater platforms to paranoid xenophobia and racism.

The days following a tragedy are pastorally crucial. One moment of crisis can provide more important opportunities for spiritual formation than an entire year of planned programs.[14] These are opportunities to teach communities how to respond to fear and violence, to learn the language of Scripture in a powerful and urgent way. When a church community learns the structure and language of biblical psalms, that language permeates our response to tragedy: personally addressing God, living in the tension of the cry of dereliction with a confession of faith, and recalling God's character in the midst of suffering. When we communally respond to tragedy with biblical lament, we "bring theodicy right into the sanctuary."[15]

Submitting to moral authority. Another important posture for believers to have toward Scripture is the expectation that it will exert moral authority over us. Many of us have been taught to understand everything in Scripture as a spiritual principle intended for our individual knowledge instead of either a redemptive story or a moral authority over us. When we lose the expectation that Scripture will convict us, discomfort us, and direct us on moral issues, we begin to look to other sources of moral authority.

And then if we think it has no bearing on the political, economic, or social aspects of our lives, we can spend all the time in the world under the reading and teaching of Scripture without it impacting the majority of the decisions and actions in our lives. As ethicists David Gushee and Glen Stassen explain, Christians' "ideological captivity" is often due to misplaced sources of moral authority.[16] We often relate to Scripture as merely an authority over our brains—thus a source of the right theology— and not as a powerful and living source of authority over our communal moral decisions.

Historically, this approach has been the downfall of the church in her most crucial moments. The church has become the tool of oppressive regimes throughout history, including American slavery,[17] the Holocaust,[18] and the Pinochet regime in Chile.[19] Much of this was made possible by relegating the moral force of Scripture to secondary status in favor of spiritualized truths with no application to material realities. When we lose a sense of the moral authority that Scripture has over us, we are able to isolate biblical stories from the larger narrative of redemption and are in danger of using them to justify whatever we want.

Retaining a sense of the moral authority of Scripture requires that we study it in the community of the church. When the gospel is carried by a particular people in a particular place, Christ's resurrection remains the launching point for witness, instead of "a sign or metaphor for a spiritual or moral meaning for life that is better understood when placed in another language than that of the church."[20] The church has largely adopted the modern notion that humans should all agree on "fundamental naturalistic and secular descriptions of reality, whatever religious elaborations may lie over them."[21] This notion makes the fundamentally political nature of the church difficult to sustain or communicate to a world that expects that our moral categories and questions will be entirely congruent with their own.

American evangelical faith is highly individualistic and privatized. We tend to conceive of the church as a voluntary association of people with similar values and beliefs. Instead, the church is a material reality that should resist its own "spiritualization"[22]—the taming of a living organism in order to avoid societal conflict. Political scientist Ronald Beiner argues that modernity has required that religious convictions be adapted in one of two ways: civil religion or liberalism. Either the church is empowered for the sake of creating national citizens or it is relegated to the realm of private belief and experience.[23]

Evangelicals may oscillate between these two options. On one hand, the Religious Right is evidence of the creation of a civil religion that marries limited government and social conservatism with loosely religious convictions. On the other hand, the church is depoliticized: our faith is relegated to the private sphere, and our political convictions are free to be pragmatic and morally relative. Without Scripture exerting moral authority over the church, it becomes a voluntary association united by right thinking, faith becomes a private commitment, and public morality becomes flexible. When our faith merely informs our political practices and moral habits, we are using it as one source among many, taking its truths and translating them through layers of other sources of moral knowledge.

Receiving instead of using. One of the most important postures we should have toward Scripture is one of humble reception. We are not its gatekeepers, able to digest its meaning apart from God's gracious decision to illuminate it. God's self-revelation to his people is not a gift that switches hands from him to us, whereby he gives us the rule book, walks away, and gives us full reign to dissect and reconstruct the truth we've been given. We are in continual dependence upon God to reveal himself in his Word, with the knowledge that he has commanded us to gather as his church in order to be formed in such a way that we understand it.

In *An Experiment in Criticism*, C. S. Lewis says there is a difference between using and receiving a book, an insight just as well applied to Scripture: "When we 'receive' it we exert our senses and imagination and various other powers according to a pattern invented by the artist. When we 'use' it we treat it as assistance for our own activities. . . . 'Using' is inferior to 'reception' because art, if used rather than received, merely facilitates, brightens, relieves or palliates our life, and does not add to it."[24]

We must approach Scripture with our minds and hearts, faculties given to us by God, but use them according to the pattern God has invented. In other words, we must take Scripture the way God gave it—as a story with moral authority that shapes and constitutes a particular people.

It's Not About You

Scripture offers us an opportunity to be continually reminded of the global, historic nature of our faith, but this opportunity is frequently missed. White American Christians in particular would benefit from a reminder that we are not the main characters in Scripture. In fact, we are greatly removed—culturally, historically, and geographically—from the Scripture that is supposed to structure our lives.

The use of the original languages in our churches—whether in sermons, Bible studies, or Sunday school classes—can serve as a necessary reminder that the Scriptures we hold in such high regard were written in and to vastly different cultures, contexts, and languages.

Spending more time in the Old Testament and reading the New Testament in light of Jewish culture and practice at the time reminds us of our indebtedness to a people and culture not our own. Most of us who grew up in the church first learned about Scripture through pictures, videos, or felt boards with characters that did not correctly represent biblical characters' ethnicities. Those early representations stay with us for a long time, coloring our understanding of Scripture in ways we may not even be aware of.

When we are faced with powerful political stories that thrive on instilling fear of other people—especially those of other ethnicities or religions—accurately representing the biblical narrative is a political act.[25] We worship a Jewish, Middle-Eastern, refugee who lived and taught in a time and culture vastly different from our own. The church can immerse us in an alternate story that forms our loyalty to a church that spans history and the globe—and that will change our political as well as our spiritual lives. We will think differently about foreign aid when no nation is "foreign" to the family of God. We will think differently about refugees as we dwell on the position our Savior occupied. We will become more concerned about injustices the world over as we enlarge our sense of the kingdom of God. One of the most important reminders for the white American church right now is that we are not the original beneficiaries of this message, who then benevolently spread it to the unchurched nations. We are the "ends of the earth" (Acts 1:8), not the main characters in the story.

One of the most difficult assumptions for children of liberalism to unlearn is that individuals are rarely the main agents or audience in Scripture. It's much easier to read statements about poverty, prejudice, and racism as politically neutral when we assume they are intended to be understood and applied by individuals instead of communities. "What does this say to the church?" might prompt a different answer than "What does this say to me?" We can miss judgments made on entire communities for perpetuating unjust systems, or exhortations to care for the vulnerable as communal efforts.

How Matters as Much as *What*

I began to see the things I'd been missing in Scripture during my second year of seminary, when I spent a semester exegeting Ephesians 2 in one class and preaching on it in another. Living in Dallas, a city with a long and complicated history of racial division and violence, the truth of some of the verses in particular took on new meaning. A text that was explained to me as a purely spiritual reality uniting two people groups with religious differences—Jews and Gentiles—turned out to be a radical statement about racial, social, and cultural division.

> For he himself is our peace, who has made the two groups one and has destroyed the barrier, the dividing wall of hostility, by setting aside in his flesh the law with its commands and regulations. His purpose was to create in himself one new humanity out of the two, thus making peace, and in one body to reconcile both of them to God through the cross, by which he put to death their hostility. He came and preached peace to you who were far away and peace to those who were near. For through him we both have access to the Father by one Spirit. (Ephesians 2:14-18)

My exegetical work in one class made it clear—this passage had significant implications for a divided nation, but it also had significant implications for me as a white student on a divided seminary campus. A *New York Times* article had just come out detailing the exodus of many black Christians from white churches in the Dallas-Fort Worth area, as political and cultural divisions ramped up and many no longer felt safe or at home in their own churches.[26] In the face of silence by many white churches on horrific instances of racism like the KKK rally in Charlottesville, black Christians felt betrayed, ignored, and unloved.

When it came time to take the theology I had learned in one class and turn it into a sermon outline for another, I couldn't help but think about segregation. The people in my class were students at a seminary with a long history of segregation, both legal and cultural. When desegregation in public schools began in the state of Texas,

Dallas Theological Seminary, as a private institution not yet required by law to integrate, was pressed on its policy. The official stance was to avoid the controversy entirely, because, as former president John D. Walvoord said, "The Scriptures never discuss the matter of segregation. . . . There is nothing in the Bible which deals with the subject."[27] And so it wasn't until 1973, after years of claiming to be open to all applicants but receiving only a handful of black students, that the administration openly said, "Dallas Seminary welcomes black students."[28]

What does this have to do with how we read and interpret Scripture? I realized as I prepared my sermon for this class that it might be too easy for myself and many of my fellow students to brush off our past and pretend we could never make the same mistakes. After all, we knew the Bible so well we could never fall into thinking it didn't say anything about racism. But this would be simple hubris, looking back on our leaders and thinking they had it all wrong and that we knew better now. Likewise, not only do white Christians need to take more responsibility for our own history and the way that it informs our own prejudices, but we need to understand how easy a mistake this was to make from a position of power and privilege. Furthermore, failing to see how much Scripture has to say about racial violence and injustice is easy when we aren't listening to or learning from black Christians.

For students at a seminary that takes pride in prioritizing the exegesis of Scripture, missing something this theologically fundamental suggests we aren't attending to our blind spots. If a prominent leader, someone who knew the Bible incredibly well and taught it for years, can miss something like this, so can we. One of the most political acts we can do is to push back against the homogeneity of privileged perspectives and seek to learn from the kind of voices the Bible is full of—the marginalized, vulnerable, or oppressed.

A Last Example

Perhaps the most recognizable instance of historic misuse of Scripture in America is the defense of slavery. Historian Mark Noll uses a volume of sermons published in 1861 to demonstrate this point: the book, *Fast Day Sermons: or, The Pulpit on the State of the Country*, included ten sermons from nationally prominent church leaders defending or condemning abolitionism. As Noll notes, the striking thing about the collection is the universal "respect for the Scriptures as providing a standard of divine truth for the orientation of human life as a whole."[29] Sermons with completely opposite positions exhibited similar hermeneutical principles and a stated reverence for Scripture.

Noll outlines some important reasons for this tension, including the "heretical hubris of American exceptionalism," fallen human nature, and the inherent difficulty in applying biblical truth to different circumstances and cultures. One of his points, however, is especially important for our purposes here. Noll argues that the "persistent problem of Protestant biblicism" creates an inability to recognize or address cultural influences on our interpretation—both the ways that these influences will predispose us to certain conclusions and how these circumstances may require different application in different cultures or time periods.[30] This is usually combined with hermeneutical naivete—our persistent claim that the Bible has a plain meaning universally accessible to everyone in all cultures and from all backgrounds. Instead of recognizing our own biases, the need for thorough study and learning from others, and our displacement from the histories and cultures of Scripture, we insist that we can just read the words and have sufficient understanding. Reading Scripture with the recognition of our own biases, humble engagement with the global and historic church, and special attention to marginalized voices will transform us and our churches.

6

Ekklēsia

THE CHURCH AS A TRAINING GROUND FOR
POLITICAL ENGAGEMENT

*The church is not a soul-rescue depot that leaves us to muddle through
the regrettable earthly burden of "politics" in the meantime; the church is
a body politic that invites us to imagine how politics might be otherwise.*

JAMES K. A. SMITH

*They are all defying Caesar's decrees, saying that
there is another king, one called Jesus!*

ACTS 17:7

A friend recently confided in me how much he was enjoying his
new church, because, he said, "They don't get all political." He was
leaving a church that had tightly welded themselves to conservative
politics, and he was relieved to attend a church that didn't have an
identity based in political positions.

In that sense, he was right to be relieved. But it's hard to imagine
how any church—a group of people who gather because of their identity
as an outpost of a coming kingdom and their commission to serve the
true king—could truly avoid getting political.

Politics is not the muddy underbelly of human existence, the unfortunate reality we endure in spite of our heavenly future. And yet even when we put political engagement in its rightful place and guard against it being either our ultimate hope or our doomed fate, it's still easy to neatly section it off from the domain of church worship.

So far, we've explored the ways that political participation is deeply formative, affecting not merely our political positions but our theological convictions and spiritual formation. We've also explored the ways that political participation is a gift and obligation, a way to love our neighbors and steward creation. These two positions produce tension: political participation is dangerously formative, and yet it is one way we creatively pursue the common good. How do we participate in politics without being malformed by it? We need to counteract one powerful source of formation with something stronger.

If we are called to engage in politics, and yet this engagement endangers us in so many ways, then there must be something about our worship and practice as believers that protects us and sustains us. Far too many conversations about Christian political engagement miss the heart of the question, which is also the heart of the Christian life: the church. Our greatest political identity is our belonging to the people of God, and our handwringing over the state of Christian political engagement today would be better served by going back to the original source: the creation of a new body politic, an embassy for the kingdom of God, the community of citizens who serve another king.

Strangers and Sojourners

Prior to the question of political engagement is the question of what I mean by "church," and why it's important to root our spiritual and political formation here. The church is a community of the people of God (Hebrews 4:9; 11:25; Revelation 21:3), created by the new covenant (Jeremiah 31:31-34) and the outpouring of the Holy Spirit (Acts 2; 11:15). The church is a material reality, not just a collection of like-minded people who fulfill their individual obligations with each other nearby. Dietrich Bonhoeffer put it this way: "The church does not come into being through people coming together . . . it is in being through the Spirit which is effective in the community. So it cannot be derived from individual wills."[1]

The church is, in the words of the Apostles' Creed, "the communion of saints." It is a particular people, "strangers and sojourners" (1 Peter 2:11 TLV). It is not a building, a denominational affiliation, a national or state church, or a group of people who join the livestream of a popular church service. It is a political institution eschatologically oriented toward the redemption of all things and a social witness to that reality (Matthew 11:5; Romans 8:22). It is commissioned by God as the mediation of his mission and blessings on earth.

The church is the body of Christ—the united flesh that Christ nourishes and cares for as someone does their own body (Ephesians 5:28-31). The church is also the body of Christ as it physically represents him on earth, having been empowered to participate in the same work he did while here.[2] This picture of the body of Christ is what encourages us to understand the church as united in her diversity, including members with different functions and gifts all in service to the whole (1 Corinthians 12:1-31).

This is important because American Christians in particular have a bad habit of seeing the church as extraneous to their spiritual lives.[3] Shifting theological tides toward inner transformation and classic liberalism's impulse toward separating the private and the public combine to leave no room for the church—it's neither public nor private, and it's an accessory at best to our private convictions. When the church becomes accidental to Christianity, the weekly gathering becomes merely a social opportunity to confirm our prior personal experience with God. We've lost the sense of the church as the center of our corporate identity because we've lost a sense of any corporate identity at all.

The church is nurtured as a particular people by its practices: corporate worship, the sacraments, spiritual disciplines, and community. These practices form us into the kind of people suited to fulfill our commission to make disciples, witness to the coming kingdom, and live for the life of the world. Low-church evangelicals like myself may be accustomed to treating what we do on Sunday morning with a certain level of inattentiveness: the important thing is the preaching, and everything else we do is more about personal preference. We can become largely unaware of just how important everything else is for our spiritual formation.

As Annie Dillard expresses it, "The churches are children playing on the floor with their chemistry sets, mixing up a batch of TNT to kill a Sunday morning. It is madness to wear ladies' straw hats and velvet hats to church; we should all be wearing crash helmets."[4] Thinking of church this way, our practices and the way they form us are dangerous things—and if we deny this reality, we're revealing how little we think they have the ability to change us and the world. And if the church is truly the center of our Christian lives, our corporate practices are particularly dangerous.

The *Ekklēsia*

The use of the word *ekklēsia* is our first indication that this community is a political one. It is "striking that the earliest Christians chose a distinctively political . . . term for their collective existence, speaking of themselves as an *ekklēsia*, a public assembly, rather than as a 'religious gathering' ('synagogue')."[5] It would be strange to eschew the private connotation of a word meaning "religious gathering," especially in an incredibly pluralistic culture. The chosen word has an explicitly public connotation: in "refusing the available language for private associations (*koinon* or *collegium*)," the church was saying that it was not "gathered like a koinon around particular interests, but was concerned with the interests of the whole city, because it was the witness of God's activity in history."[6]

Rather than being the center of believers' political identities in the sense that they learn how to advocate for narrow interests and fight for "their team," the church is gathered as a people who have all of creation as their horizon of concern. The church is a political body in that it is interested in the common good and not in the sense that it is a political party with members to represent. After evangelical flagship magazine *Christianity Today* published an op-ed by editor-in-chief Mark Galli supporting President Trump's impeachment, the president tweeted that the magazine was looking for Democrats "to guard their religion" and that "no President has ever done what I have done for Evangelicals, or religion itself!"[7] It not only revealed the president's view of his relationship with evangelicals but highlighted the attitude many evangelicals share: Christians make political decisions based on what will protect them and their interests. But the church is commissioned to seek the flourishing of our communities, not special privileges for ourselves.

I share Stanley Hauerwas's desire for the church to be "a body constituted by disciplines that create the capacity to resist the disciplines of the body associated with the modern nation-state."[8] In other words, if the church is intended to be an alternate community that witnesses to a better kingdom and a better king, it needs to work to live out that community in the midst of political forces demanding ultimate allegiance. The church is political not because she is isolated from the earthly nation she inhabits but because she refuses to entirely abdicate the realm of political action and formation to the state.

Jonathan Leeman calls the church an "eschatological embassy."[9] The church is not the state, and it is not commissioned with the same mission or given the same authority. Nor is the church in the business of policing the rest of the world. When Paul tells the Corinthians to expel wicked people from their community, he explicitly mentions that it's not their business to judge those outside the church (1 Corinthians 5:12-13). The church is not a community you enter by virtue of where or when you're born or who your parents are. The church is an embassy because, while it is a political community, it is an outpost in foreign territory, a representative of a coming kingdom living in the midst of the current one.

This is why it's helpful to talk about the church as an institution. Christians are often quick to contrast the relational family of the church with heartless and bureaucratic institutions. But as Jonathan Leeman notes, even if the church is a family, community, or a people, it's still an institution.[10] Any community that operates on the basis of a particular set of beliefs and shared rituals is an institution. It takes people from their prior social constructions and gives them a new set of rules to operate by.

There's a popular quotation from the Dutch Reformed theologian Abraham Kuyper that frequently pops up in political conversations: "There is not a square inch in the whole domain of our human existence of which Christ, who is Sovereign over all, does not cry 'Mine!'" As Jonathan Leeman notes, this rightly understands Christ's lordship as universal, but is "institutionally unspecified."[11] What does it mean for government institutions, farms, universities, families, and churches to operate under the lordship of Christ? God does not seem to require the same things from each of them.

Understanding the church as an institution helps us think about its jurisdictional limitations. It is one institution ordained by God, and government is another. Where we draw that line is complicated, but understanding each institution as both ordained by God and limited in its authority is a helpful place to start. These limitations create room for neutrality without declaring one institution completely uninterested in the activities of the other, and vice versa. The church and state are limited in their authority, but that doesn't mean that either are politically or spiritually neutral. The state doesn't have jurisdiction over worship and theological convictions, but its actions are theologically significant; likewise, the church doesn't have jurisdiction over legislative matters, its actions are politically significant.

One way Christians have historically understood the relationship between these institutions or spheres of authority is by sharply differentiating between them, giving an exclusive list of authorities to the church and an exclusive list to the state. Instead, an account of the political nature of the church requires that we understand this division as temporal, not spiritual versus material, or inner versus outer. Temporal authorities have power given them by God, but that power is dependent upon him as its source, and its time is ending. The problem with theories that harshly distinguish between the political and ecclesial spheres is that in separating theology from politics, they create a political ethic untethered to theological considerations.

Instead, we can understand the relationship between church and state authorities as a difference in time: one is fading away while the other bears witness to a coming reality. This temporal government is not replaced by an apolitical reality but by a truer political reality, one in which humans exercise their creative capacities in total freedom and righteousness, unconstrained by our own sin and by the powers and principalities operating in a fallen world.

Paul's missionary journeys were so disruptive to the cities he entered because he was not merely a spiritual leader offering a new religious organization to join or experience to pursue. Instead, he entered political arenas as "an ambassador for a king-in-waiting, establishing cells of people loyal to this new king, and ordering their lives according to this story, his symbols, and his praxis, and their minds according to his truth."[12] When you understand the social and political implications of the gospel, the Great Commission ends up looking very much like the original command to rule and reign over the earth. The church is not peddling religious experiences; it is capturing the loyalties and affections of a people who serve their king by stewarding his creation.

A Moral Training Ground

This is why understanding the material reality of the church is a prerequisite to any conversation about Christian political engagement—we aren't a loose collection of individual believers with individual callings. We are a people with a commission to seek the flourishing of creation. If the church is an "eschatological embassy"—an outpost of another kingdom living in occupied territory—then its work in the world must begin with the training of its people.

Understanding our churches as training grounds for engagement with our communities will change the way we worship together. Our corporate worship trains us in a story and then sends us with that story into our various manifestations of worship—in our stewardship of earthly resources, in our care for the vulnerable, in our cultural creativity, and in our responsibility to the communities we live in. Ellen T. Charry describes classical theology's view of moral formation as requiring "emotional engagement with concrete models for emulation and a social context within which to practice them."[13] This understanding of our commission and obligation reorients our corporate experience. We need opportunities to rehearse moral skills, tell stories that reflect our commission, and reflect on how our failure to practice these skills is met with God's grace. Again, we are not isolated individuals striving after kingdom ideals; we are the people of God, given gifts that equip us for our still imperfect but blessed work in the world.

Our corporate worship is what Episcopalian bishop Charles Chapman Grafton called "the school of our affections."[14] We learn what to love and how to love it through our communal participation in the practices of the church. No part of this equation can be divorced from the rest without harm: it is about our practices, our community, and our affections. Jonathan Edwards's language of "religious affections" remains popular today. While Edwards's use was focused in explaining what true conversion looks like, his language is appropriate for what we mean here. Affection is the motivation for enduring persecution and difficulty, it is produced by faith alone, and it is rooted in the soul but expressed in the body. He describes our affections as particularly strong and somewhat involuntary inclinations toward certain goods—we do not necessarily logically deduce what to love, but we are drawn to it because of our affections. That is why he can say, "True religion, in a great measure, consists in holy affections."[15]

Affections is an appropriate word because it makes no divide between the social, economic, political, or spiritual. We love what we learn to love, and we love those things in all different spheres in our lives, in many different ways. Our love for the widow, orphan, and foreigner does not have boundaries when it is an affection that has been nurtured in physical, emotional, communal practice. It is not a position we have been invited to hold, but a love that is deeply rooted in us.

This is one reason Stanley Hauerwas has famously said that the church does not *have* a social ethic, it *is* a social ethic.[16] There is no real divide between worship and ethics, liturgy and politics. We do the things that we affirm together, sing together, and perform with our bodies. The very concept of *applying* our theology to our politics reinforces the liberal notion of private religious convictions versus public civic engagement. We don't cultivate private beliefs and ideas in the shelter of the church and then tiptoe out into the public square with them held tightly in our hands, trying to use their power but denying their presence in our lives.

Corporate worship is the center of our political engagement because it is in this context that we learn how to live the lives that God asks of us. Corporate worship teaches us to focus our ethical judgments on God's moral framework. It teaches us what rhythms of life God has created for us, and it teaches us how to treat our neighbors. If we are interested in resisting the modern liberation of politics from theological constraints, then our worship should politically educate us—by teaching us about what kind of people we are, the redeemed creation we are awaiting, and how to expectantly await it.

The Old Testament details Israel's long history of detaching politics from theology and receiving God's condemnation for it. The prophetic literature in particular is rich with warnings against religious ceremonies undertaken in the midst of blatant social injustice. Just as Isaiah 1:10-17 was referenced in chapter one, Amos describes Israel's religious practices as a stench that God will not accept and their songs as noise that he will not listen to (Amos 5:21-23). Instead, this is the command: "But let justice roll on like a river, righteousness like a never-failing stream!" (Amos 5:24).

It might be the most common perversion for God's people: to expect our religious devotion to excuse our injustice. Yet Isaiah 58:3-7 rebukes God's people for fasting and thinking that he will notice their devotion while they spend their fast days exploiting their workers, fighting, and striking each other. These are sobering words from the prophet: "You cannot fast as you do today and expect your voice to be heard on high" (v. 4). Instead, this is the kind of fasting God has chosen: "to loose the chains of injustice and untie the cords of the yoke, to set the oppressed free and break every yoke" (v. 6), to "share your food with the hungry and to provide the poor wanderer with shelter" (v. 7).

In Jeremiah's temple sermon in chapter seven, he calls out the people for thinking they're safe from God's judgment in his temple, that their outward acts of devotion should protect them from the consequences of their sin. Instead, Jeremiah tells them the conditions for their safety: "If you do not oppress the foreigner, the fatherless or the widow and do not shed innocent blood in this place, and if you do not follow other gods to your own harm, then I will let you live in this place, in the land I gave your ancestors for ever and ever. But look, you are trusting in deceptive words that are worthless" (Jeremiah 7:6-8).

There are differences between our religious and political obligations today and those that were given to Israel as God's national chosen people. But the point that they needed constant reminding of is the same one we need drilled into our heads today: our religious activities are worthless if they aren't causing us to live and act justly. God does not divide between justice and worship.

And yet even when we are struggling against our injustices and idolatries, there are deep structural factors we feel powerless to change. Instead of being a reason for abandoning our responsibility and throwing our hands up in the air in defeat, the gross systemic injustice in our world is even greater reason for submitting to the forms and practices God has given us. As Ephraim Radner says,

> We don't have time in our hands—time to make the changes we need to make in order to convert cultures, historical diseases, and so on—but God does. We do not have the power any longer to embrace a culture as a whole with our religion and so, in a deliberate squeeze, to transform it—but God does. We do not

have the focused Spirit to quench the passions of human hatred that poison even the heart of religion—but God does. What we have are the forms that tie themselves to God's time and to God's power and to God's transformation. We have such forms, and whoever we are, and to whatever church we belong, we can submit to them.[17]

Sacraments

Of all these "forms that tie themselves to God's time and to God's power and to God's transformation," there are two that truly constitute the community of God's people. If we are going to discuss how the church itself is the training ground for our political engagement, the sacraments—the practices that usher us into the community and the practices that sustain that community—are the only place to start.

Our discussion of both sacraments faces a similar problem—these are two of the most divisive areas of Christian theology. How we practice and think about baptism and the Eucharist places us in different traditions and denominations. It would be easy to assume that this reality makes the sacraments too complicated a subject to see universal truths about Christian practice and political engagement. My goal is to describe both sacraments in ways that believers with a variety of perspectives on these issues can both agree with in some ways and perhaps be challenged in others.

Baptism: the naturalization ceremony. Baptism is the sacrament that most fundamentally constitutes this community. In an individualistic culture and a fragmented world, baptism is a physical and visual reminder that the church is a real, material community. During a discussion about the necessity of baptism in one of my seminary classes, this question was posed: "Let's think about a Christian community undergoing persecution in a nation where the Christian faith might get you killed. Official entrance into the Christian church could cost you your job, family, or life. Do you continue baptizing people?" The question rightly noted the privilege American Christians have to practice our faith freely, but it also revealed how little we have to lose when we enter into the Christian community via baptism.

For many American Christians—regardless of their view of baptism but particularly for credobaptists—the sacrament is an outward reflection of something internal, a confirmation of a prior reality, a moment for the family of God to affirm the defining beliefs of their family. If we understood the church as a material reality, a community created by the Holy Spirit and not by our willingness to drive to a building on a Sunday morning, we might view our entrance into that community as more materially significant.

In class that day, all I could think about the question was: Do we understand what our baptism *should* cost us? If we understood our baptism as ushering us into a new community with demands on our time, money, political priorities, and family, would we think it was just as dangerous for us? While our baptism certainly affects us in a different way than it does persecuted Christians around the world—and American Christians do have unique privilege in our country—do we really believe that our baptism could cost us our lives as well? Or are our churches living in such a way that would never disrupt our cultural, economic, and political systems?

Baptism is a naturalization ceremony, initiating believers into their new citizenship, publicly declaring them members of the new covenant community and enlisting them into the mission of the coming kingdom of God. Baptism gives tangible and visible form to a community that stretches across history and the globe. Instead of signaling another commitment among many others we may make, "baptism is the formation of a new people whose newness and togetherness explicitly relativize prior stratifications and classification."[18]

Baptism creates a community of equality in a world of injustice. In 1978, Richard Mouw wrote a straightforward defense of the political nature of baptism, particularly in the context of racial issues. In what I'm sure was a controversial first sentence at the time—or might be even today—Mouw says that his congregation recently "issued another declaration on race relations. We do this kind of thing regularly these days. As far as I can tell, there is never a dissenting voice. The entire congregation just speaks out in unison and commits itself to the cause of race relations."[19] What "declaration" is he referencing? The recent baptism of a young black man into the congregation.

Mouw argues that when a congregation receives this young man, they are committing to understand how the gospel impacts the various social and political dimensions of his life and to treat any affront to his dignity as an affront to the entire community. "If American society tries to treat him like a second-class citizen, we will have to protest on his behalf, since he is our brother in a holy nation of kings and priests."[20] There is no long train of expositional gymnastics required here: our community is constituted by a ritual whose very essence is egalitarian.

In the early church, baptism into a new community had radical social and political effects. It meant that people living in wildly different social categories shared the same value and significance as brothers and sisters. Unity is conferred in baptism in the way a legal status is conferred upon a new citizen. Differences are not abolished; they are relativized and reorganized around this new identity. But it doesn't mean that this experience in the church leaves the divisions and inequalities outside of the church community ignored. As Christians experience a remarkably different political community and the unique demands of its citizenship, their imaginations should be opened to a new kind of politics and its redemptive potential.

What a radical difference it would make in our communities if we were given the political imagination that baptism is intended to give. In the culture and politics that the early church was born in, everything revolved around the Roman "domination system": there were the rulers and the ruled, and your identity was based in who you had authority over and who had authority over you.[21] It is in the midst of this cultural reality that Jesus institutes an initiation rite that relativizes all of these power relations and flips the order of obligation and authority upside-down. In Matthew 28:16-20, the resurrected Jesus appears to his disciples and gives a remarkable commission to his followers: with all authority on heaven and earth (v. 18), Jesus commands his disciples to make disciples "of all nations, baptizing them in the name of the Father and of the Son and of the Holy Spirit" (v. 19).

In an American church culture full of language about the Great Commission and foreign mission trips, we may miss the most politically significant part of this command. These are the same nations that Rome had ultimate authority over. The disciples are in effect being told, "Therefore go and make defectors." Their commission is to beckon Roman subjects to a new allegiance, a new kingdom, a new king. From the very beginning, baptism is associated with the kingdom of God and the resurrection of which Jesus is a first fruit.

Perhaps the most dangerous thing a person in the Roman empire could do is pledge allegiance to a political radical who was executed by imperial authorities. "What could be less patriotic and dishonorable,"[22] asks R. Alan Streett, author of *Caesar and the Sacrament.* "Stratification was an essential part of both Roman and Jewish society, and everyone knew their place and functioned within those limitations. But in the kingdom of God slaves could serve as elders, women could prophesy, and Jews and Gentiles were equals. The Christ movement, operating as an alternative polis potentially threatened Roman social stability."[23]

The New Testament says remarkably little about baptism, which makes its clear focus all the more important: unity. The second half of 1 Corinthians 12 is popular for its description of the church as a body— ears and hands are reminded that they all serve crucial but different parts. But this section begins with an important basis for this unity: "For we were all baptized by one Spirit so as to form one body—whether Jews or Gentiles, slave or free—and we were all given the one Spirit to drink. Even so the body is not made up of one part but of many" (vv. 13-14). We are one body in Christ because we have entered into this community the same way—not of our own merit but because of the Spirit.

Baptism enlists us into a community that supersedes all other loyalties, and some of our confusion lies in misunderstanding what the church is and our obligations to it. Baptism ushers us into a community that serves a different king and rehearses the practices of another kingdom. When the patriotic, security, and prosperity gospels come knocking, our baptism should be like the passport that lists our proper identity in the face of the values and ideals of other kingdoms.

The Eucharist. Like baptism, the Eucharist creates an equal community in a world bent on hierarchizing. One of the few places in Scripture that deals with the sacrament is a rebuke to Christians who would use it to reify the inequality of the surrounding culture. In 1 Corinthians 11:17-34, Paul has incredibly harsh words for the church at Corinth. He says that their meetings "do more harm than good" (v. 17)—in the early life of the church, Paul tells a congregation that their practice is so wrong it would be better if they did not meet! Their wrongdoing is this: there are divisions among them (v. 18) and the result is that "it is not the Lord's Supper you eat" (v. 20). The material inequality between members of this community and their replication of cultural expectations about wealth and privilege meant that they were "guilty of sinning against the body and blood of the Lord" (v. 27).

It would be easy for us to look around our churches on a Sunday morning during Communion and pat ourselves on the back because our churches are tight-knit communities with minor conflicts that get resolved in a healthy manner. And yet the social inequalities that Paul condemns so harshly might be more visible in our church services than in any other part of our social lives. The divisions in our churches extend beyond specific congregations; they are manifested in the reality that most of our churches are filled with people who look just like us. In a country with a deep and long history of racial injustice, our churches have represented the status quo or worse more often than they have represented a prophetic challenge to it.

Even in the basis for our practice of Communion there is an explicit connection to the way the sacrament reorients our relationship to politics and power. The Last Supper in Luke 22 is quickly followed up by

Jesus' words about political power and abuse of authority. Jesus gives the words that many of us hear every week:

> And he took bread, gave thanks and broke it, and gave it to them, saying, "This is my body given for you; do this in remembrance of me."
>
> In the same way, after the supper he took the cup, saying, "This cup is the new covenant in my blood, which is poured out for you." (Luke 22:19-20)

Then he says that someone at the table will betray him. In the resulting discussion, the disciples begin fighting about which of them would be considered the greatest.

In the immediate conversation following Jesus' words of sacrifice and humility, his disciples begin squabbling about who will be more important. Jesus' response connects the significance of the Eucharist with the repudiation of power politics: while he has just displayed his laying down of ultimate power for the sake of others, he tells them that the "kings of the Gentiles lord it over them" (v. 25). But for those who follow this sacrificial leader, he says "the greatest among you should be like the youngest, and the one who rules like the one who serves" (v. 26). In receiving the Eucharist, we are rehearsing a story about the values of the kingdom of God, values that are completely contradictory to the surrounding world. In a culture obsessed with hoarding power, the church meets to practice a symbol of strength in weakness.

The Eucharist is truly a political act, particularly in a world where food itself is political, caught up in important questions about economics, poverty, cultural exploitation and appropriation, and human bodies. It's especially relevant when you consider the context of one of the few descriptions of the actions of the early church in the New Testament. In the second chapter of Acts, we are given this picture of the new church's life together: "They devoted themselves to the apostles' teaching and to fellowship, to the breaking of bread and to prayer" (v. 42). Their religious practices—teaching, fellowship, Communion, prayer—are described

right before the description of wonders and signs (v. 43) and their economic practices: "All the believers were together and had everything in
common. They sold property and possessions to give to anyone who had
need" (vv. 44-45). The very next verse mentions Communion again.

Sandwiched between mentions of the early church practicing Communion is the reality that they also practiced their life together—with
deep economic implications. It would be too much to say that this
commits believers to a particular economic program, but it would not
be too much to say that it entails a commitment to sharing and stewardship, of advocating for the needs of the marginalized and impoverished, and pursuing economic justice. Our life as a community cannot
help but be impacted by the realities of wealth and poverty, excess and
hunger—especially when our central communal practice deals with the
earthly substances of bread and wine. Our community-defining practice
is constituted by the building blocks of human life—sustenance often
denied to other image bearers.

The Eucharist should spark in us an eschatological imagination that
envisions the day when everyone receives the nourishment they need.
The reality of "world hunger politics—especially the denial of access to
food for everyone for the sake of securing the wealth of the rich countries of the Northern Hemisphere" is the greatest challenge to this
vision.[24] The biblical witness is filled with examples of God's provision
for his people, often symbolized and actually provided by food. In the
exodus, God provides manna that spoils when his people hoard it. In
Acts 6, food distribution is unequal, and the solution is to elevate the
marginalized in order to ensure justice. In the midst of a world taken
over by the logic and language of the market, in the Eucharist we take
one of the most foundational human needs and give and receive it freely,
reminding ourselves of our eschatological vision of abundance instead
of scarcity.

The Eucharist is also a reminder for the self-sufficient and triumphalist American church that we are not only dependent on God but also
dependent on the total sacrifice of Christ. The Eucharist fosters in us a

dependence upon God that should push back against our impulse to trust in economic systems that provide for us at the expense of others.[25] In all the places where we are tempted to put our faith in earthly institutions to protect and provide for us, our practices are meant to expose them as powerless: all we have on earth is what we receive from Christ.

The Eucharist should instill these values in us. It should form us in particular ways and orient us to the abundance and justice of the kingdom of God. And yet, as evidenced as early as in the church at Corinth, it is often perverted. One powerful meditation on this reality in more recent history is William Cavanaugh's *Torture and Eucharist*, about the Catholic church and the Pinochet regime in Chile. In the early days of the military regime, patrols roamed the streets looking for those labeled enemies of the state. Three days after the coup, two young leftists decided to try to run and arrived at the door of a priest's home in the center of Santiago. They were allowed inside but not permitted to stay. So later that evening "as the community prepared for Mass, a seminarian spoke up and objected to the celebration of the Eucharist under the circumstances. He said Christ had been turned away at the door of the residence. Communion in the body of Christ had already been denied in the denial of the two seeking asylum."[26] The more that we grasp the significance of Communion in our own communities, the more we will notice the absences and denials that pervert it.

Our consistent failure to receive the Eucharist in a church devoid of injustices and failures could lead us to abandon it or its political significance. And yet this feature of the sacraments—their ability to be twisted and corrupted—is actually another important political reminder for an American church drunk on triumphalism. Our worship and our political engagement share an important feature: they are but glimpses and shadows of an eternal reality, and continuing to do the work keeps us hungry for that reality. Both sacraments keep us waiting for the ultimate fulfillment.

We can't change all the surrounding divisions, legal and cultural, that make our gatherings completely unrepresentative of the true diversity of the body, but in our gathering our hope is its own kind of defiance: "while the faces and colors of our gathered congregation might constantly remind us that the kingdom remains to come, the Spirit also invites us to overcome, reminding us that, despite the failures internal to our gatherings, at the same time the worldwide chorus looks miraculously like this kingdom choir."[27] Our failures are both impetus to reform and reminder of our finitude. We cannot master every political obstacle on this earth, and we will consistently fail to be the beacon of hope and unity to the surrounding world that we intend to be. And yet the very feeling of absence of brothers and sisters should remind us of an eternal hope we wait on and a reality we are called to strive after in this life.

Where we might be tempted to cordon off our practices from the political realities under which our neighbors exist, the Eucharist should remind us of the material reality of need, scarcity, and injustice in our world—and the sacrifice Christ made to one day bring total justice and redemption to our broken world. The rules of engagement that the world offers—survival of the fittest, winner takes all, cutthroat competition— lose all significance at the table. We are confronted with the reality that our victorious Savior bought our freedom with sacrifice and weakness and has called us to resist the power politics of the world for the sake of the world.

The Body and Bodies

Of the many overlapping themes between baptism and the Eucharist, there is one we can spend years in church without noticing, and yet it is one of the most politically important. Both sacraments require our bodies—hands that guide another's body into water, hands that break bread, teeth that chew, throats that swallow. In a world of increasingly online churches—internet campuses, live-streaming services, or even an entire church on an app—the church's constituting practices still require our bodily presences.[28]

Many of the churches I grew up in talked about our bodies like they were unfortunate realities we were stuck with for this travail on earth.

I still remember giddily recounting a youth group sermon on heaven to a friend who was spending the summer losing weight with me. "One day, we won't have bodies to hate!" Our church rarely practiced Communion; and when we did, we spent just as much time explaining that the material elements themselves didn't matter as we did actually passing the trays of bread and grape juice.

The fact that the constituting practices of the church are firmly rooted in physical realities has great political import. Spiritual practices rooted in physical habits remind us of our identification with the material suffering of the world. "What more than the human body and its needs makes us present in the world?"[29] Virtual or internet church may be a beautiful use of technology for disabled or marginalized people, an opportunity for long-distance connection to a home church, or reaching those who would otherwise never darken the door of a church. But the loss of physical presence is a cost so high that it should be nothing but occasional when necessary.

Many of our churches act as if what we do in our communal gatherings is nothing but a barely physical reminder of totally spiritual realities. This thinking seems to go that if physically gathering becomes inconvenient, we'll stop, because the heart of the service is the inner experience of individuals, not the material reality of the church practicing her bodily sacraments in the physical presence of the community. But our God incarnated among us not just to identify with our physical bodies but to bodily inhabit the good creation that had been corrupted and to call us to a coming kingdom that would take one shape among many as a new heaven and new earth we inhabit with resurrected bodies like Christ's own.

Political Training Ground

Our conversation about Christian political engagement must begin in the church, because all conversation about Christian life begins in the church. When we primarily think of our faith as a personal relationship with Jesus, we will view church like any other social group—another opportunity to meet people with common interests. Our political engagement will become a personal issue where we untangle social and cultural issues on our own, taking inner convictions and translating them into personal activism. Instead, the most politically significant aspect of our faith is the reality that it is birthed and nurtured in an alternate political community that serves another king and awaits another kingdom. Jesus wasn't making converts—individuals who would pledge their individual support of him as a religious leader—but citizens of a new kingdom.

THE **Rhythm** OF **Our Lives**

TIME, MUSIC, CONFESSION

We keep a troubled vigil at the bedside of the world.
We cannot accept its sickness as unto death but we cannot grasp
the meaning and the hope of a cure that will make life all about us hale
and well. The contemplation of the destruction of the world at our hands
confronts even our little lives and their little part with a guilt too vast
to assuage and too overwhelming to manage. Thus we clutch the
moment of intimacy in worship when we become momentarily
a part of a larger whole, a fleeting strength, which we pit
against all the darkness and the dread of other times.

HOWARD THURMAN

I have absolutely zero rhythm. I love singing in church, but I have to concentrate really hard on following the lead of others around me, or I might sing an accidental solo. My worst fear is that an enthusiastic worship leader will play an upbeat song and encourage us to clap along, because trying to keep up with the words and claps at the same time is simply asking too much. However, most churches are small enough and quiet enough that I can concentrate on a few people to follow along with, watching their claps and actually hearing them sing along. We're all working together to follow a rhythm.

The sacraments are the identity building blocks for the church, practices that remind us who we are. And most of the other things we practice corporately enforce this identity and remind us of our mission: our calendar, music, confession, architecture, and service. They create the rhythm we follow, a model for our lives that we begin to naturally fall into after much practice. These practices are politically significant in their own unique ways that we'll soon discuss, but they all share this important element with the sacraments: they form our loves and loyalties to our rightful king and the inbreaking of his kingdom. They teach us what kingdom living looks like—not by handing us a list of rules, worldview points, or instructions to memorize, but by teaching us a rhythm to fall into.

Just like the sacraments, these practices take on a myriad of forms in different communities. The music we sing and the buildings we worship in will look different depending on the denomination, tradition, or surrounding culture of the church. And yet each of these discussions is intended to both further identify us with our particular local community and yet shape that identity in line with the global historic faith, the universal, (lowercase c) catholic church. I think William Cavanaugh said it best when he noted that in church worship, the "global and the local are refracted in such a way that one becomes more united to the universal the more one is tied to the life of a particular local community."[1]

Time and Our Collective Memory

There's something everyone in my seminary community starts saying at the end of the spring semester. "It's April." You don't have to explain what it means, because it has taken on a universal meaning. It might even be your sole answer to the question of how you're doing—it means, "Busy. Tired. Stressed." "It's April" is code for "that time of the year when everything is due, the whole campus is stressed, and everyone is on the verge of an existential crisis." We've marked this unique time by the month in which it all happens, and like clockwork, April comes around, and we all feel the weight of its meaning.

Most of us experience something like this as the year passes by: January means a new beginning, August is for beach trips, September is for freshly sharpened pencils. The rhythm of the year brings with it certain smells, sights, and sounds. The church has its own rhythm based in the church calendar—a guide for God's people to rehearse its story and reinforce its identity.

Robert Webber, in his fantastic introduction to the church calendar, *Ancient-Future Time: Forming Spirituality Through the Christian Year*, gives this wonderfully simple explanation of the basis of the calendar:

> The saving deeds that God accomplished in Christ are historical events. They are not mythical ideas or powerful stories but true, real, concrete events through which the God of creation acted within history to rescue the fallen world. The very heart, center, and focal point of all God's saving activity is the passion and resurrection of Christ. Consequently, the very heartbeat of time, the source of meaning and power for the cycle of all time, derives from and returns to the death and resurrection of Christ in which God was uniquely active reconciling us to himself (2 Cor 5:18).[2]

The church calendar leads the community of the people of God through his story, which has become theirs. Yet the calendar is not just historical education or a tool to teach the Christian story. The calendar powerfully forms our loyalties to the global community of faith, transcending national or ethnic allegiances. Following the liturgical calendar reinforces the sense that we are bound, even in our marking of time, to a different family and citizenship than those that vie for our highest loyalties here on earth. Our modern conception of history as "additive"—the sum is no greater than the parts; events are just arranged on a line of time without a necessary relationship—was required in order to create the modern nation-state. In order to foster a strong loyalty among people who might not share values or culture, this conception of time bound people together who share time and geography. In opposition to this conception of time, the church understands herself now as having "an imagined contemporaneity among God's people stretching from the biblical world to the present."[3] Yet our modern loyalties are often most greatly formed toward those geographically or temporally close to us, instead of to the global and historic church filled with the people of God, with whom we have more in common.

The church's ordering of time also has deep political ramifications—from our thinking about foreign aid to our advocacy for refugees to our general approach to foreign policy. While elected representatives are responsible to constituencies in a special way, Christians have a different set of responsibilities—to a people that does not follow the same categorizations that create nations and interest groups alike. When communities come together every week and rehearse a story and follow a calendar that people across time and space have also rehearsed and followed—it should shape our identity and mission in a countercultural way.

Fostering an identity that spans time and space will look different for marginalized peoples than it should for majority culture Christians. This shift toward identifying more strongly with the global, historic faith provides necessary correctives for Christians who benefit from their identification with cultures, countries, or people groups with power. For Christians from oppressed communities, these instructions could come across as an attempt to rip them away from supportive communities and force solidarity with people who have historically perpetuated their oppression. I can't prescribe what this idea will look like in those communities, but I believe it will look more like taking comfort in the historically and geographically diverse expressions of Christian faith as counterexamples to majority culture expressions of Christianity. For both the powerful and the marginalized, the reality that our faith is bigger than particular expressions of it should change us, albeit in different ways.

The church calendar also gives us an important means of understanding and living in God's story now. Many preachers make God's sovereignty a central part of their message without giving that sovereignty the shape and meaning it deserves. If we aren't careful, we can use "sovereignty" to baptize any unjust political or social reality.[4] But rehearsing God's story through the church calendar gives us a tangible picture of God's presence in human history—a progression of redemption that is inherent to his sovereignty. When we narrate the past through God's redemptive project, we understand the grand sweep of his story and remember the particular ways he inhabits the supposedly random events of nations and kings—not by sanctioning all of human history but by sometimes quietly and imperceptibly working through it for his own purposes.

It's helpful to imagine history as a woven tapestry, as theologian Laurence Hull Stookey does.[5] On the side presented to the world, there are mostly green vines and leaves, with an occasional yellow bud. These small flowers are much less prominent than the green that covers most of the tapestry—from the presenting side, the green is telling the main story, and the pops of yellow are minor and random. But if you turn the tapestry over, you see that in order for those little yellow buds to dot the landscape requires that the yellow cover the back, woven in between everything else going on. This is what rehearsing the story of God in history teaches us to see: what look like glimpses of his power appear as his total sovereignty when you see the story from the other side.

In Deuteronomy, Moses told the people what to do when their children asked, "What is the meaning of the stipulations, decrees and laws the LORD our God has commanded you?" (6:20). And what should we do when we introduce children—for Israel, these were the only people who would not know God's requirements—to the way of life God has commanded of us? We tell them a story, similar to the one Moses provided as an answer for the Israelites: "We were slaves of Pharaoh in Egypt, but the LORD brought us out of Egypt with a mighty hand. Before our eyes the LORD sent signs and wonders—great and terrible—on Egypt and Pharaoh and his whole household. But he brought us out from there to bring us in and give us the land he promised on oath to our ancestors" (6:21-23).

When people enter into the community of the people of God, we don't just teach them doctrine. We tell them a story, we practice living into that story, and we follow that story with our calendar. For example, Webber says of the early church's celebration of Easter that "this early Christian feast was no mere recollection of a historical event as an end in itself. Like the Jewish Passover Seder, it recalled an event to transform life."[6] We are changed by the time we inhabit this story because, as does all of our liturgy, the Easter story teaches us what to love, long after, and emulate. Children exhibit this human tendency so beautifully: when you tell children stories, they don't just want to hear them told again and again (though they want this too), they want to act them out, take their place in them, and rehearse their own imaginative retellings. Some adults grow up and do this through fan fiction—when you love a story so much that you aren't content to just heard it told and retold, you want to inhabit it, taking the pieces and reimagining them in your own context.

Each of the "gospels" we described in chapter three have their own sacred calendars—ways of marking time that tell the story of the community of their adherents. The prosperity gospel is marked by New Year's and its resolutions to work harder and be better. In America, the patriotic and security gospels are marked by similar days—the Fourth of July and its promise of national glory, Presidents' Day and our myths of America's inception, and Veterans Day and its story of military sacrifice and success. They each combine to create the liturgical year for the average American: days marking significant communal history, but also often solidifying our consumerism, exceptionalism, and pride. The church calendar reminds us that our lives today should be ordered differently from the rest of the world.

Sometimes the church calendar seems unnecessary to Americans because we think we live in a Christian nation. Instead of recognizing the way this overlap has warped our observance, however, we view it as another reason that our life as a church community is not so different from our neighbors. In a piercing insight, theologian Martin Connell argues that "American anthropology is reflected in how its churches keep time."[7] Probably the greatest example of how this has actually harmed our observance is in our national recognition of Christmas. He notes that Christmas is the only religious holiday that marks the year for virtually all Americans, and consequently, this makes it the only church event that marks the passing of time for many Christians. We celebrate Easter, but it doesn't often form the foundational structure of our year the way Christmas does. Our churches more easily follow the cultural lead of the nation when we lose the sense that there's a difference at all between our identity as Christians and our identities as Americans.

Cultural expressions of the Christian faith will vary, but this example gives us some insight into how our distinctive practices could better shape our political and social lives. When we don't perceive our communities as following a different marking of time in line with a different story, we lose some key distinctives of our faith. Connell notes that "U.S. Christians prefer the shining star over Bethlehem to the blood and guts of Gethsemane and Calvary." A church more formed by a national calendar than a Christian one may rejoice in a miraculous birth, but it will not have space for a crucifixion—or the self-denying ethic the resurrection would justify. If our churches were as marked by all stages of the church calendar as we are by the single consumeristic pull of Christmas in the Western world, perhaps we'd be less triumphalist, less concerned with putting on appearances of success and wealth, and more aware of the deep comfort our faith offers to the suffering.

There isn't room here to go through each of the church calendar seasons, but here are two short examples of how learning to tell time in the church forms us in politically important ways in these specific seasons.

Advent

Unlike the consumeristic advent of hurried shopping, weekends stacked with parties, and pacifying our impatience with chocolate calendars, the Christian Advent is a somber reflection on the already-and-not-yet.[8] We are in the unique position of living in between two Advents, celebrating the incarnation and yet longing for the second coming. There's something important about Advent distinct from Christmas—instead of merely celebrating the first coming as a way of anticipating the second,

Advent focuses our attention on the darkness and brokenness that make us desperate for the final redemption of all things. There's even a sense in which Advent allows us to grieve our waiting, crying out to God and admitting that we often doubt he's ever coming.

In her book *Advent: The Once and Future Coming of Jesus Christ*, Fleming Rutledge beautifully describes this tension. As the early church continued to wait for Jesus' return, anxious and desperate in the midst of persecution, they began to wonder if he was really coming back at all. "And in its perplexity, the young church repeated a story to itself,"[9] Rutledge says, then recounting a story told by Jesus in Mark 13. Jesus said, "It's like a man going away: He leaves his house and puts his servants in charge, each with their assigned task, and tells the one at the door to keep watch. Therefore keep watch because you do not know when the owner of the house will come back—whether in the evening, or at midnight, or when the rooster crows, or at dawn. If he comes suddenly, do not let him find you sleeping" (Mark 13:34–36).

The owner of the home is away, but "it is he who put the whole operation in motion, who gave shape and direction to its existence." And then Rutledge reveals the full force of the story in light of Advent: "The expectation of his return is the moving force behind all the household activity, and yet often it seems that he will never come."[10] There might be nothing more radical and politically important than the notion that we are both anticipating the coming kingdom of God and offering glimpses of it today. This posture of waiting and hastening (2 Peter 3:12) is a necessary stalwart against both political idolatry and political apathy. Instead of using the coming reign of Christ to justify political inaction, exploitation of the natural world, and indifference toward material suffering, Advent reminds us that we still have a job to do. While the master of the home is away, the expectation of his return motivates our participation in the redemption of the world. At the same time, the Advent reminder that we live between two advents keeps us from putting our hope and salvation in earthly political systems, for our true king is coming again and possesses the real power to make all things right.

All Saints' Day

All Saints' Day, which is observed in Protestant churches on November 1, commemorates some historic figures of the church as the Catholic celebration does, but it's more often about the people in particular congregations who died that year. In a way even more concentrated and powerful than the church calendar as a whole, All Saints' Day reminds us of the reality that our family spans time and space, generations and cultures. It offers an opportunity to grieve, and soberly remember our own human finitude. As G. K. Chesterton is remembered saying: "If you want to know the size of the church, you have to count the tombstones."

All Saints' Day doesn't let us get away with ascribing faithfulness to worldly measures of success, because the wealth and power that hold sway during one's life hold no significance in death. It might seem strange to say that remembering and dwelling on death has any political significance. Yet our churches have historically been formed by our awareness of our frailty, our weakness, our smallness. In countries where our faith has lost the cultural position it was born into—persecution and marginalization—we need to be more conscientiously reminded that our faith is more attuned to suffering than conquest. More immediately, it gives us an opportunity to grieve and to grieve with those who grieve in a way that our characteristically peppy church cultures don't always make space for.

The Church Calendar as Rhythm

The early church's entire life was centered around a new timeline—a new day of gathering (Sunday), and a new order to the entire year. The church calendar reflects this reordering of time. "The early Christian calendar enabled the church to see time as a medium that belongs to God and unfolds according to God's purposes."[11] Time is not neutral, and neither was it determined by the rituals and festivals of the Roman world that the church was born into. The process of "Christianizing the calendar" took centuries, precisely because the rhythms and rituals of the pagan calendar were so deeply entrenched in the surrounding culture of the early church. Those rhythms and rituals formed people toward a particular end, and the eschatological orientation of the church required a different set of rhythms and rituals to counter them.

As does all our liturgy, the church calendar forms in us a "feel" for the world, a story that narrates the hard edges and sharp corners of our experience. Like every other observance or practice of the church, the goal here is not to draw a straight line between our worship and particular political positions. The problem is deeper than that. Our fundamental orientation to the world is in need of repair and falling into the rhythm of the church teaches us to navigate cultural and political positions with the right perspective. If we learn the story of God's redemptive work in the world, we will find our place into the story instead of clinging to political idols or short-term solutions.

Rhythm-Making Practices

The rhythm of the life of the church is important because, like the Christian story, it orients us to the world. When you have lost your step and can't find the road ahead, the rhythm invites you back into the way of life that you have learned, that is still familiar, and that other people are following. Like the calendar, these are practices that shape our loves and loyalties at a subconscious level, continually pulling us back toward a particular vision of common good and a story of creation, fall, and redemption.

Music. The songs we sing together are strongly formative—they shape the language we reach for in times of suffering and rejoicing, they prepare our hearts for other forms of worship, and they require the use of our bodies (throats and mouths to sing, hands to clap or play instruments). As John D. Witvliet says, "Dieticians have taught us to live by the maxim 'We are what we eat.'" We recognize the incredible power of the food we eat to change our bodies and our lives. Similarly, music "has the uncanny ability to burrow its way into our spiritual bones. When it comes to matters of spirituality and faith, we are what we sing."[12]

Like all worship, the songs we choose to sing communally should teach us of the cosmic scale of redemption. In the summer of 2018, I traveled to Cebu, Philippines with My Refuge House (MRH), an organization that provides long-term aftercare to restore survivors of commercial sexual exploitation. I was given the opportunity to witness the work of this organization, meet their local staff, and celebrate their ten-year anniversary. Our small group was not necessarily there to serve the girls (MRH recognized the difficulty associated with short-term trips like ours) but to witness the redemptive work happening on their campus and use our gifts and resources to support them.

The anniversary celebration included a performance by the girls for local guests—partners of the organization, friends, family members—of a popular worship song. The lyrics powerfully describe God fighting for, chasing down, and rescuing "me." There is incredible truth in the song: God really does leave the 99 for the one. He wants his children to experience individual redemption. And yet hearing this song took on a new and uncomfortable meaning for me in Cebu. In an American church service, the lyrics fit right in. My sins separate me from God and I need person reconciliation. But as I listened to the girls practicing—in a home created to restore survivors of an evil system of sexual abuse, in a country marked by colonial exploitation—the same lyrics rang hollow.

We spent a good amount of our trip learning about commercial sexual exploitation: how it is often fueled by poverty and a lack of education, how government corruption exacerbates it, how different regulatory and policing solutions have failed. In this context, a focus on *my* sin and *my* redemption felt woefully inadequate. These girls faced systemic evil, and I wanted desperately to believe that God would do more than light up my own darkness or defeat my own lies; I wanted him to defeat poverty, corruption, and the pervasive culture of sexual abuse.

If "we are what we eat" applies to the songs we sing, we have an overly individualistic diet. Many of the songs sung in evangelical churches focus on individual salvation rather than cosmic redemption. We conceive of the power of Christ's redemptive work on the cross in largely individual terms, which leaves us with largely individual concepts with which to think about our lives and work in the world. If the only real problem is the hearts of fallen people, we will rightfully evangelize and disciple people but neglect to address the systemic forces that keep them in poverty or oppression.

The songs we sing day in and day out shape our moral and political imagination so much more deeply than a sermon that addresses a political issue or a Sunday school class that decides to discuss a cultural problem. But there also exist these key moments in the life of a congregation where pastors and worship leaders have a unique opportunity to shape their congregations. In moments of great fear or instability, the music we sing has incredible power to return to us and offer empty relief or deep comfort. Matthew Kaemingk gives this powerful example of imagining churches around the country gathering to sing "O God of Every Nation" after 9/11. The hymn begins,

O God of every nation,
of every race and land,
redeem the whole creation
with your almighty hand.[13]

The rest of the hymn uses clear language to address the threat of fearful division when tragedies strike. And these beginning lines exemplify the kind of posture that our communal songs should teach us—that our God is sovereign, that his community spans nations, and that we await his final redemption of all creation. The way we respond to wars, natural disasters, and terrorism is indicative of where our loves and loyalties lie: where we seek hope, who we protect and who we vilify, and the avenues we use for expressing our fear and pain. The songs we sing together as a community in the aftermath of those moments have the power to confront the sinful impulses of our hearts and direct our fears and desires toward their rightful focus. At times when we are tempted toward xenophobia, militant self-protection, or fearful scapegoating, the language we have learned through rhythm and repetition should return to us, forming us into a people who cry out to God to heal creation.

Pastors and church leaders can instruct their congregations in the cosmic scale of redemption or the appropriate response to a tragedy, but that instruction pales in comparison to the impact of music. The songs we sing become the language we use, the posture we have toward the world, the rhythm that shapes our lives. We rarely remember sermons, but find ourselves humming the song we sang on Sunday.

Buildings and programs. Unlike some of these other rhythms, our use of our church buildings is not some existing practice we need to reemphasize or practice differently. I'd like to suggest that we ought to rethink our buildings and the way we use them for the sake of a right understanding of the role of the church in the world. If we seek formation in the direction of better loving our neighbor, we will learn to see our church buildings and resources as conduits to the good of our communities and gain a greater understanding of the practical needs of our communities. Instead of living as isolated church communities, we can open our buildings for others to use toward the flourishing of our broader communities.

I have a pretty sporadic schedule of hours at my church—as part-time staff, I'm in my office a few hours a week, in Bible study or a church service for a few hours on Sundays, and in meetings in classrooms a few hours in the week. Whereas many members of our congregation only come in the building in their designated times—a Wednesday night Bible study, Sunday service, and so on—I see what happens in our building at "off" times all week long. There are two different minority communities that hold services in the building (a Chinese and a Pakistani church), Alcoholics Anonymous meetings on Thursday nights, and a Boy Scouts troop that built a new stage for our children's ministry in the same room they meet in every week. I am continually thankful to serve in a community that refuses to hoard our resources but instead chooses to give them away to churches launching, organizations seeking the good of our surrounding community, and other groups needing space. There are dozens of considerations for every particular church community to consider in the use of their building, but one way that we could embody and teach our mission as the church for the life of the world would be to hold our buildings with open hands.

There's another unexpected benefit to this approach: when we open our buildings to other groups, we may find ourselves unable to host as many programs for the church itself. If our spiritual formation includes our participation in public life, we might not seek to fill families' calendars with church activities but instead equip them—including children and teenagers—to live more faithful lives outside our walls. Like each of these suggestions, what this looks like in particular contexts will vary widely, but this posture—of seeking the flourishing of the community by offering use of our buildings—could be a fruitful start for creative reimagining of our own spaces. Perhaps as we slim down our programming we may even find ourselves returning to a truly multigenerational community, the kind where a Sunday service includes elder generations on down to screaming babies and wiggly toddlers.

Suggestions such as these—letting "outside" groups find belonging inside our buildings, seeking worship with our whole families—should form us in the direction of holistic care for the community. When kids from other churches use our classrooms, when families from the community feel at home in our building, and when a bored kid disrupts the service, we might begin to learn that there is really no such thing as "other people's children."

Confession. Practicing confession together should teach us that corporate, generational, and systemic sins exist and require corporate repentance. If we say together that we have "left undone those things which we ought to have done," we may begin to see how we are implicated in apathy that's even greater than ourselves—that is, political apathy. When the church asks for forgiveness—from each other as individuals and from the world as a people—it reminds us of the deep and insidious evil around us and our own susceptibility to it. When we as a people are in regular practice of admitting where we have been wrong—morally, factually, accidentally—we put into practice what we believe about our lives in this fallen world and prepare ourselves to offer contrite hearts to it. The church is a community that knows how costly forgiveness is and confesses to believe in the great depth of depravity in the world. When we practice confession, we are making ourselves a people formed by forgiveness and able to more robustly engage the evil in the world.

In her essay "Repentance as Political Witness," Jennifer M. McBride argues that much of our polarization and division comes from increasing triumphalism—the arrogant confidence in our own beliefs—and, I would also argue, in "our people" or "our side." She argues that the best witness the Christian church has to offer is a nontriumphal witness, because "the flourishing of the common good in our pluralistic society demands a humble witness, and even more, faithfulness to the character of the crucified Christ demands a humble witness."[14] Our communal repentance can create in us the right disposition toward our own sin and acknowledgment that we have been complicit in injustice in the past and are susceptible to it in the future. McBride argues that a larger pattern of speaking and acting constitutes real repentance, as well as concrete engagement that arises from taking responsibility for the part we play in structural injustice and systemic sins.[15]

Yet by contrast, the tendency of most American Christians seems exemplified in the attitude of the Religious Right: "Christians who deemed themselves morally elite citizens called by God to combat the 'godless elite'"[16] instead of recipients of unmerited grace. McBride sees this same tendency in the progressive evangelical movement, but with substituted moral and political issues. The desire for a prophetic witness is a righteous one, except when it comes from a place of triumphalism, as if Christians have some moral high ground to recapture in the first place. The problem with both views is that they presume "the church is specially positioned as judge over society,"[17] instead of inextricably bound in society, guilty of complicity, and often a leader in immorality.

When we confess together, as a community, we are reminded that none of our sin is truly personal or individual. We are implicated in patterns of sins natural to our culture and community, we are impacted by the sins of others, and we benefit from systemic sins we didn't personally commit. As with each of these suggestions, corporate confession isn't a magic pill that fixes our individualistic mindset or immediately awakens us to our privilege. But also like each of these suggestions, its slow and consistent integration into our lives will very often have an effect on us. The more my awareness of my individual sin is brought into the realm of the community, the more I may find that no sin is truly only mine. Within the community of the church, my particular bents and habitual sins affect others, and their sins affect me. With this perspective, perhaps we'll be aware of how this remains true in our wider world as well.

Preaching. For most American evangelicals, putting preaching last on this list will seem strange because we see preaching as the centerpiece of our corporate worship, the real reason we gather every week. While this focus is not without merit in an increasingly biblically illiterate culture, it is last on this list precisely because our focus *is* so squarely on this means of corporate worship, education, and edification. And yet none of these other practices is complete without good preaching. Preaching gives words and thoughts to the actions and bodily postures we practice, it explains the rituals we participate in, and it illuminates the story of the church calendar.

Preaching forms the church as a political community by the stories it tells, preaching being "the proclamation of reality."[18] When we listen week after week to the story of a coming kingdom and the defeat of the powers and principalities, it will change us as a people. Preaching takes the storytelling at the heart of every other practice of the church and declares that the story is reality. Preaching has the potential to not only repeat the story but also challenge the hearers to believe they have a part to play in the story, a vision of the future to live into, and a rich history that they can claim as their own.

Part of the political significance of preaching, however, comes about when a preacher is willing to allow Scripture to convict and discomfort rather than encourage or uplift. One of the greatest roles of the preacher is to help the congregation situate themselves in the text. For example, week after week, are we learning to see ourselves in the role of the oppressor and sinner who needs grace and responds with repentance, or do we learn to come to the text expecting to see ourselves in the role of the beleaguered righteous? We may find ourselves represented in different positions at different times, but the white American church in particular needs preachers who are willing to situate us in the place of the privileged and powerful and to take on ourselves the associated judgments. Do we have ears to hear every instance where the prophets condemn our religious ceremonies in the midst of injustice?

Scholar and preacher Tim J. R. Trumper contrasts apolitical and partisan-political preaching with "biblical-political" preaching that neither becomes entangled in partisan concerns that overshadow the spiritual meaning of the text nor loses the cosmic transformation of the gospel in order to avoid political concerns.[19] Preaching does not need to be overly concerned with political education, but it does need to be courageous enough to resist the temptation to shy away from the political implications of the text.

Not Like It's Supposed to Be

A friend of mine recently confessed that he and his wife had spent the last year at a liturgical church that he loved while she withered. We were both in the midst of classes and research that was leading us further into a love for liturgical expressions of the faith and the conviction that propositional education was not nearly as powerful as bodily, sensory ritual. And yet just as he and his wife returned to the type of evangelical low-church community they'd grown up in, I was arriving at a similar question as he had: "But why doesn't it always work?"

We both had become convinced that our spiritual formation as believers was more strongly determined by stories, rituals, and communal expressions than by didactic preaching or information accumulation. But we both had also come to the uncomfortable realization that this wasn't a magic formula. Very often an account of corporate practices like the one this book offers can assume that the practices will be performed "according to their abstract and ideal descriptions" and ignore the possibility that misperformance regularly affects the power of these practices.[20]

We will not only imperfectly perform these practices; we will often perform them according to characteristic malformations. In her important book *The Danger of Christian Practice*, Lauren Winner describes how the very nature of the sacraments and prayer have been part of their misuse—they have "characteristic damage."[21] Historically, the church has taken the very gifts God gave us in order to make us a community lived for the life of the world and has used them to exploit or oppress others. These practices have great potential to shape us into a kingdom community, an eschatological embassy that seeks the flourishing of the world as to witness to the shape of the coming kingdom of God. And yet they are human practices—human because human beings practice them, describe them to each other, and pass them down through generations.

It is not the intention of this book to prescribe particular changes in every tradition and context but to suggest to ministers, lay leaders, and Christians in all traditions that one important response to our current political moment is to conceive of these practices for what they truly are: political acts done in a political community for the sake of a political world. Looking at our practices in this light is not the sole or most important way to think of them by any means, but taking the time to evaluate them in this way should highlight for us some perversions we've allowed, some practices we've neglected, and even some ways we may be able to do them differently.

I'll give one example of a common distortion in a practice that can rob it of its power. Many evangelical low-church congregations can create an atmosphere that is conducive to individual rather than communal expressions of worship regardless of what practices are performed or introduced. When our lights and music (and maybe even a smoke machine!) create a concert-like atmosphere, we don't just provoke the ire of older generations. We create a space that, like a concert, may require the "feel" of a crowd of people but does not require that we have any relationship with those other people. As a result, we feel alone in the crowd, not part of a community. When we sing "together," receive communion, or pray in this atmosphere, we lose some of the communal power of this practice.

There's another uncomfortable answer to the "Why doesn't it always work?" question. The reality is that when it comes to injustice, there are two sides of the same coin: while these practices are intended to shape us into a justice-seeking people, they are also less and less effective when we are actively perpetuating or benefitting from injustice. As Nicholas Wolterstorff explains, if we worship but neglect acts of mercy and justice, "a shadow is cast over the worship, and its authenticity is brought into question."[22] This is a prominent theme in Scripture—our actions lose their effect and purpose when they are done absent a struggle for justice. The ethical life of the community impacts their worship (Amos 5:21-24; Isaiah 58:3-7; Isaiah 1:11-17, 27; Jeremiah 7:1-11; Micah 6).

Our attempt to explain the political power of these rituals and practices is not an attempt to artificially attach a convenient meaning that isn't otherwise there. If we try to do that, it will either fall flat by itself or by virtue of the inauthenticity of our attempt. But the worship of the church, its practices and habits, and its very existence are all inherently political. The issue is not in finding politically relevant ways of worshiping or reconstructing what we do so that they meet a foreign goal. Instead, we're meant to make explicit the places in our worship and identity that the church is missing or ignoring in this unique political and cultural moment.

There's a reasonable critique of this approach that would argue that by turning worship into a political, moral, or ethical act, it undermines our right focus: praising God. Our focus should not be on what worship does to us but on how we communicate our praise to God. But for Christians, worship is not merely an outburst of praise to God. It's a command and calling he has given his people—a command that takes a particular shape, forms them in a particular way, and has intended consequences for the whole world that witnesses it. In worship, Christians "experience the presence of the acting and judging God in a formative way; and here, at the same time, a reflective ethics will emerge among them—social behaviour guided by 'the law of the Spirit' (Rom 8:2), a form of living which takes in all the different sectors of existence."[23] In other words, our corporate worship shapes our worship out in the world.

The frustrating reality is that what is supposedly implicit in the liturgy is difficult to communicate or reveal to a church so deeply formed by political practices outside of the church. Our reevaluation of our practices in this light can be helpful, as can an attempt at making too-familiar practices unfamiliar again. One of my favorite things about studying Scripture in its original languages is how unfamiliar it makes the text. Passages and verses that are incredibly familiar to most believers become unintelligible at first and then slowly more understandable. There have been simple phrases or sentences I've heard in English a thousand times in my life that, once I'd put in the hard work of translating them from Greek or Hebrew, became startling unfamiliar and surprisingly beautiful again. Perhaps one way of refreshing our understanding of these practices is to make the familiar strange again so that they can become familiar in a new way. Or for other people and churches, it could require stripping back our attempts to normalize practices that are intended to be strange so that we become comfortable with what is strange, in order to become a strange people.

Yet in the midst of all of this, we must remember that worship is not a "linear, harmonious socialization process, in which the ethical shaping of believers follows like words written one after another on a blank page."[24] This is not a formula: worship this way and you will get results. More than misunderstanding the process, expecting these kinds of results this drastically misunderstands our own power. These forms of the church, these habits and practices that shape us into people who witness to the coming kingdom, are given to us precisely because we are weak and small, vulnerable to perverting or misusing these gifts. We were not given formulas or programs but prayer, the sacraments, preaching, music—all things that are hopefully pushing us further into a recognition that God is the one who works in us, who fights the powers and principalities, who forms us into a visible expression of his rule on earth.

8

Bent ON THE Coming Kingdom OF God

SPIRITUAL DISCIPLINES AND POLITICAL FORMATION

*Through activism we confront toxicity in our world; through
contemplation we confront it in ourselves.*

PHILEENA HEUERTZ

Some of us are particularly drawn to the idea of spiritual
disciplines—and not just because we grew up learning about them or
witnessed their regular inclusion in the life of the church. Some of us
are drawn to the spiritual disciplines—or rather, the concept we think
lies behind them—because they represent formulas that turn us into
better people.

Personally, I like results. I like knowing that I can do the right things,
plug in the right variables, and get the right outcomes. And when it
comes to spiritual disciplines, the results are our own inner transformation. In this way of thinking, our growth and development as Christians is not out of our control; it is something we can work hard at and
guarantee results. Kyle David Bennett says that this understanding of

the disciplines thinks of them as "divine opiates" that help believers reach "spiritual euphoria."[1] We want to know the trick to being a better Christian, to finding inner peace, to getting rid of our pesky temptations and sin patterns, and the spiritual disciplines come along and seem to promise a formula for achieving results.

Yet just as church worship is not a linear progression, a formula in which we plug in the right cognitive understandings, actions, and practices and out pops the right political posture, the spiritual disciplines aren't static formulas that we can manipulate and control any way we want. And just as church worship is not primarily about our inner experience of satisfaction or peace, the spiritual disciplines—the patterns and practices of believers in the church—are aimed at creating disciples in the world, not highly spiritual people who want to escape it.

We're distinguishing the disciplines because they are in a sense individually practiced, not because the things we do corporately are for the sake of the church and the things we do individually are for our own sake. Spiritual disciplines are practices for a community to reform its way of life together, to individually practice the story that we tell corporately, to put in place habits and postures that make every area of our lives look more like the shape of the kingdom of God we proclaim together in worship.

Frederick Buechner says that we "carry inside us a vision of wholeness that we sense is our true home and it beckons us."[2] And there is a sense in which these practices are about us as individuals, but they are also forming members of a community, parts of a whole, people whose sense of identity is wrapped up in the kingdom that the church witnesses to. The work of the disciplines *is* largely internal—they shape our desires, loves, joys, and dreams for the future. But they are also external in their outworking—they are intended to affect our actions, convictions, and the way we operate in the world. Our corporate worship rehearses this story together, and our spiritual disciplines internalize that story in our minds and bodies so that the vision of wholeness we learn together is carried with us into the world.

There are obviously ways in which every spiritual discipline—a tricky designation anyway—could and should have political effects, in the sense that everything we do as humans (and especially as members of the political community of the church) has political effects. The following examples are either disciplines we could think about differently in order to more fully realize their political effects or disciplines we usually neglect that have particularly important political effects.

Prayer

Prayer is the foundation on which all the other disciplines rest—it centers our attention on God, asks him to direct our desires, and places us in a state of dependence and humility. In and of itself, prayer has deep political effects—we recognize that we are dependent upon God for everything we are and have, a dependence that destructs liberal notions of autonomy and self-sufficiency. If prayer is a true encounter with the living God, the God who commands his people to seek justice and protect the vulnerable, this encounter should shape us into a people who witness to his character and follow his commands.

There are plenty of reasons that this discipline often fails to live up to this reality. In *The Dangers of Christian Practice*, Lauren Winner's chapter on prayer centers on the written prayers of slave-owning women in the antebellum and Civil War-era South as modes of household management. These women knew the centrality and power of prayer and used it to ask for obedient slaves.[3] As broken, fallen creatures we will not only ask for things that go against the character of God, we will often practice the discipline of prayer in a way that forms us to believe God is on "our side" (as white people, Americans, or Westerners). We might not seek control by our own actions, but we will continue to seek social and political control through the prayers we pray. Not only does a proper theology of prayer help fight against this reality, but a renewed practice of prayer is required.

One of my favorite stories in all of Scripture is the story of the unexpected faithfulness of Ruth. Contrary to its popular conception as a sweet love story or as merely a foreshadowing of Christ's role as kinsman redeemer, the book of Ruth is about how God worked in the life of a marginalized person—a Moabite woman—to continue David's line. Perhaps the most convicting truth in the whole book comes in the middle of the strange story about how Ruth lay at Boaz's feet and asks him, "Spread the corner of your garment over me" (3:9). If you read this story as a love story, Ruth makes an awkward and gutsy request. But if you read it as the story of a faithful young woman who fights for her vulnerable mother-in-law with everything she's got, you'll get a bit of a different take.

Earlier in the story, Boaz recognizes Ruth's work ethic and blesses her, "May the LORD repay you for what you have done. May you be richly rewarded by the LORD, the God of Israel, under whose wings you have come to take refuge" (2:12). A chapter later, Ruth essentially asks Boaz to become the answer to his own prayer: he asked for her to be richly rewarded by God, to be protected under God's wings, and then she asks him to spread his garment over her. These two words in English, *wings* and *garment*, are the same Hebrew word, *kanaph*. These two signs of protection are vastly different; God's protection is infinitely greater than what Boaz can provide. And yet we're supposed to connect these two "wings," these two descriptions of protection. This is the part of Ruth's story that we would all do well to learn from: if we're going to pray for God to protect and provide for the foreigner, the widow, and the vulnerable, we should also be willing to be the answer to our own prayers.

How can our corporate and individual prayers reflect this reality? Certainly we'd need to begin by consciously evaluating what we pray about and how it reflects the biblical commands to care for the most vulnerable among us. This alone makes a massive difference: Are we conscious of the needs around us, and do we not only tell the Lord of our concern but confess our frequent apathy and ask for greater compassion? Beyond that, do we pray with the explicit expectation that we may be asked by God to be the answer to our own prayers? Too many of us pray prayers for protection and provision for the marginalized and then refuse to help when the marginalized turn to us and say, "Okay, can you help?"

On the other hand, prayer keeps our justice-seeking in its proper context: reliance upon God, the only One who can truly bring justice and the One who loves it more than we do. Not only does Jesus explicitly tell the disciples how to pray—more on that in a minute—in Luke 18 he tells them a parable "to show them that they should always pray and not give up" (v. 1). The parable tells of the constant pleas of a widow to a wicked judge for justice, pleas that go unanswered until she wears down the judge by her persistence. And Jesus tells them, "And will not God bring about justice for his chosen ones, who cry out to him day and night? Will he keep putting them off?" (v. 7). This is not merely a story contrasting the reluctant justice of a corrupted human judge with the perfect justice of God. It's a reminder that our persistent pleas for justice are not in vain, even when earthly forces do not respond, or respond for the wrong reasons. Justice feels far off most days, a hope so distant that we're either tempted to place the weight of securing it here and now on our own shoulders or give up on seeking it all together.

We pray with persistent hope in the face of injustice on earth, with the certainty of God's justice. Our prayers should put us in the posture of expectant hope, willing hands to work here and now, and peace that ultimate justice is already promised. By submitting our pleas for justice to both earthly judges and the ultimate judge, we are formed both to desire justice on earth and not to presume we can create it ourselves.

The Lord's Prayer

One crucially important aspect of reforming our prayers is to focus our attention to the prayer Jesus commanded us to pray—it is not free from the potential to be abused, but it is remarkably resistant to it for a couple important reasons. First are the prior instructions given in Matthew 6:5-8: a warning against hypocrisy and a warning against trying to obligate God to our needs. While the particular concerns—the public prayers in the synagogues that sought to gain public approval, and the influence of pagan practices of prayer—may or may not resonate with contemporary concerns, the commands are crucial. Our prayers are not about us, they are not for us to gain favor with people, they must be consistent with our lived actions (the opposite of hypocrisy), and they must be made in humility.

The Lord's Prayer is immediately and undeniably communal, for "Even to pray this prayer in private is to pray a corporate prayer, for we do not address God as 'my Father,' but 'our Father.' We do not pray for 'my daily bread,' but 'our daily bread.'"[4] We are not alone in our relationship with God, giving voice to private desires that do not affect others; we are communing with the God who makes us into his people, the God who hears the prayers of all of us together—including those in the family of believers who look, speak, and act differently than us. We do not approach God with merely individual concerns and praises, but with the heart and voice of a community.

The Lord's Prayer is also a political manifesto: *your kingdom come, your will be done, on earth as it is in heaven* (Matthew 6:10). We declare in every prayer that we are seeking, supporting, and desiring another kingdom and asking the king to bring it to fruition. Kingdom language can get cliché when we treat it as an analogy for Christian values instead of a literal kingdom we are tasked with witnessing to and awaiting. And the very next line reminds us that while we wait for this kingdom, we live in a broken world that does not work the way it should, because many people today are hungry, and others have too much. *Give us today our daily bread* (v. 11). While dependence on God is our eternal reality, we are awaiting the end of the current reality of scarcity in some places and extravagance in others, of some who grasp for crumbs while others hoard resources. The Lord's Prayer puts us in the right posture to address this reality: asking God to provide and reminding ourselves that even in our supposed self-provision we are truly dependent upon him.

And forgive us our debts, as we have also forgiven our debtors (v. 12). We ask for forgiveness not merely to gain a personal sense of inner peace but as a reminder that we are forgiven, called, and equipped for a purpose: to be reconcilers in this world, merciful and justice-seeking. *And lead us not into temptation, but deliver us from the evil one* (v. 13). A translation like this one reminds us of an important reality: we are not merely surrounded by vague, undefined evil. We are living on an earth captured and illegitimately ruled by an active force of evil, a power at work in the world. When we keep our confessions and our pleas for deliverance in the context of powers and principalities, it becomes increasingly difficult not to see the way that evil worms its way into our structures and institutions just as much as it does our own hearts.

The Lord's Prayer doesn't just remind us of our posture and our reality, it obligates us. We should not be able to pray with earnestness a prayer that we are not willing to let make demands upon our life—our time, finances, resources, and relationships. When we choose to repeatedly pray this prayer—on a regular basis, in times of stress or need, in moments when we do not know what to do—we are formed toward the shape of the kingdom in a way that has deeply political effects.

Sabbath

Early in my time in seminary, I accidentally stumbled into a group of writer friends. One semester we decided to take a writers' retreat and hole up in an Airbnb for a long weekend to get work done. But when you've been working hard all semester, a little break seemed too precious to give up, and we ended up spending the mornings lingering over coffee at the kitchen table, the afternoons reading whatever we wanted, the evenings playing games and telling stories that made us laugh until we cried. One of those afternoons, after a long lunch our foodie friend had beautifully prepared, I spent hours on the back porch, facing a lonely Texas wood, reading a book I'd picked to read for fun months before (it was Fleming Rutledge's five-hundred-page *The Crucifixion*, but everyone's fun is a little different), drinking cup after cup of coffee because it was wonderfully brisk outside, and I knew we could stay up late talking and sleep in late the next morning.

In some ways, that description of what was a sabbath for my friends and me sounds very typical of our understanding of sabbath—seclusion away from everyday responsibilities, physical rest, and having fun. But in a few important ways, that weekend stands out to me as a beautiful example of how real sabbath is about delighting in God and his creation in a way that has profound social and political effects in a tired, fragmented world. We weren't coming to this place exhausted—we would have plenty of moments that semester where we would feel burnt out, but we had planned this break in the midst of our regular routines of busyness. We didn't spend the time in mindless "rest"—the kind where you binge Netflix because your brain can't handle anything else—but spent time delighting in the things we loved. We had meaningful conversations, ate delicious food that it had brought our friend joy to create, played games that required parts of our brains and bodies that seminary study doesn't, read books that we loved, and drank coffee, with sugar and cream if that's how we liked it. And the thing about that weekend that felt the truest of sabbath is that we delighted in work we had done, honored others for their work that we could now enjoy, and kept from asking anyone else to work for us.

Celebrating sabbath is not about a pious abstinence from the world, nor is it exhausted respite from overwork and burnout. Celebrating sabbath is about delighting in creation and resting in our dependence upon the Creator. Sabbath is part of the rhythm of healthy human life—working and resting, yes, but something more foundational than that. Sabbath rhythm is about working hard at the vocation we have been universally given—to steward creation, to rule and reign on earth, to follow our Creator in creating beautiful and functional things with the resources he's given us—and then enjoying it. Sabbath is not about having a vacation from your relationships but about delighting in community. Whether you understand sabbath to be a standing commandment for believers or not, its inclusion in your rhythm of life can reflect an understanding of the good created order and an important counter to a culture that has no room for the kind of rest, delight, and justice that sabbath entails.

For our purposes here, the most important aspect of sabbath is not that it thwarts workaholism or encourages delight in creation but that it creates intentional rhythms of justice in the life of God's people. Sabbath as it was given to the Jewish people, and especially its perfection, the Jubilee—in Jewish thought, seven was the number representing perfection, and the Jubilee is the Sabbath's seven-times-seven iteration—were given with the explicit intention of creating a regulative life of justice for the community. When the law is given in Deuteronomy 5, the commandment to observe the Sabbath is the longest commandment, with a particular reason given: you do not do any work, nor do your children, your servants, your animals, or any foreigner (vv. 12-14); and you observe the Sabbath because you were slaves in Egypt, and God brought you out (v. 15). In Leviticus 25, a similar reason for the Jubilee is given: while the seventh year is a sabbath year in which nothing is sown or pruned, but the fruits of the land are simply enjoyed (vv. 1-7), the year following the seventh sabbath year (the fiftieth year) is consecrated. God instructs his people to "proclaim liberty throughout the land to all its inhabitants" for each to return to their family property and their own people (v. 10). The following verses explain how the Jubilee regulates the community by preventing generational accumulation of wealth, the hoarding of resources, and the disproportionate accrual of land.

Observing the sabbath obviously does not mean that every fifty years we follow these guidelines set for Israel. But understanding how the law provided explicit rhythms of justice for the community of the people of God should remind us of how to best practice sabbath as a spiritual discipline in our lives. It is not about exhaustion-driven rest or even merely about enjoying good gifts of our Creator; it is about forming rhythms of justice—imagining a world where the systems of injustice, discrimination, and oppression are not inevitable, and seeking spaces to carve out resistance against them. The sabbath should be a "weekly reminder, to all, that injustice and inequality is to be overthrown by delight and joy. To the degree the rich and the poor, the powerful and the powerless, eat, drink, and celebrate the Sabbath, it will be impossible to conduct oneself in the next six days, as if injustice is truer than the Sabbath."[5]

Fasting

Many people today are first introduced to fasting by weight-loss companies, not the church. Intermittent fasting for select hours during the day or for a couple days during the week has become a popular weight-loss technique, while many evangelical churches are both hesitant to encourage the discipline and often use the term to mean self-deprivation of anything from television to sugar. The basic message for fasting in the weight-loss world and in the church are remarkably similar: deprive yourself for the sake of making yourself better.

We tend to think of fasting as self-deprivation for the sake of fostering dependence upon God—and it certainly can do this. Yet this understanding neglects biblical and historical ways that fasting has been intended to form the people of God into instruments of his work of justice in the world. In Isaiah, the people of God express their anger that they have dutifully fasted in expectation that God will notice their devotion and that he has not responded with blessing (58:3). God replies through the prophet that during their fasting they exploited their workers (v. 3) and quarreled with one another (v. 4) instead of loosing the chains of injustice, setting the oppressed free (v. 6), sharing their food with the hungry, and providing shelter for the foreigner (v. 7). It is remarkable to evangelicals today that the instructions to God's people are not merely to really "mean" their fasting, to make sure their hearts are involved in the discipline. Instead, God explicitly connects fasting with feeding others.

Gregory the Great noted that "a man fasts not to God but to himself, if he does not give to the poor what he denies his belly for a time, but reserves it to be given to his belly later."[6] The early church was not just in the habit of fasting for inner spiritual benefit but on behalf of the larger community. Aristides, a Greek philosopher living in the second century, wrote an apologetic of the Christian movement that listed many of the unique ways of living that the early church had adopted. He noted that "if anyone among them comes into want while they themselves have nothing to spare, they fast for two or three days for him. In this way they can supply any poor man with the food he needs."[7]

For most of us, our normal food acquisition is selfish—we don't care who made it, who suffered for it, or who we will harm by consuming it. We uncritically eat food that was made under unsafe or unjust working conditions, whether by exploited farmers in other countries or by underpaid workers in our own. We pay little attention to how our food is packaged and preserved in ways that pollute the planet. We are so distant from the original sources of our food that we don't even think to ask questions about the conditions under which the workers labored or the conditions under which animals (whom we were given dominion over for the purpose of stewarding) are raised. Fasting is an opportunity not only to sacrifice our own comfort for the sake of providing for another but also to reorient our relationship to a massive industry that affects the entire world. Fasting may cause questions to arise that we've never considered, prompt us to reevaluate our regular eating habits, or encourage us to better understand the way our food is produced.

But there is a crucially important caveat to make about fasting. Just like all other disciplines and all other church practice, it has its own characteristic perversions. In a world where fasting has deep connections to weight-loss methods (for the most part, scientifically unverified), cultural messages about beauty and bodies, and language that can be misused by those suffering with eating disorders, we have to be careful. When we talk about fasting as a means to spiritual euphoria and not a means by which the church reorders its relationship to food, community, and justice, we risk reinstating dangerous cultural messages that should have no room in the church.

Feasting

I wrote this chapter during a long weekend retreat with a group of women from my church. One night as we prepared dinner, I noticed we weren't having our normal meal—we were preparing a feast. We danced to music as we stirred big pots of sauces and pasta, sliced giant loaves of sourdough bread one of the women had baked, told jokes over chopping vegetables, and laid colorful china out instead of the disposable plates we used the night before. Before we sat down to the meal, we commemorated the night by reading "A Liturgy for Feasting with Friends." Toward the middle, it says,

> May this shared meal, and our pleasure in it,
> bear witness against the artifice and deceptions
> of the prince of the darkness that would blind
> this world to hope.
> May it strike at the root of the lie that
> would drain life of meaning, and
> the world of joy, and suffering of redemption.
> May this our feast fall like a great hammer blow
> against that brittle night,
> shattering the gloom, reawakening our hearts,
> stirring our imaginations, focusing our vision
> on the kingdom of heaven that is to come,
> on the kingdom that is promised,
> on the kingdom that is already,
> indeed, among us,
> For the resurrection of all good things
> has already joyfully begun.[8]

In a world that fosters competition by pitting the needs of some against the needs of others, feasting, much like sabbath, teaches us to enjoy creation and resist injustice and scarcity. And yet this feast with my friends was lacking perhaps the crucial element of Christian feasting: it was not given for the sake of another. We were enjoying our weekend at a large home of a member of our church—a large lakefront home with a giant kitchen and more bedrooms than we could use—and we had the financial margin to take an afternoon off of work, spend gas money to drive to the home, and attend a church with a budget for a weekend of nice meals. There is nothing wrong with these joys, and there is a lesson to be learned from the generous family that used their gorgeous home to bless small groups from our church instead of protectively hoarding it. And yet our "feast" that evening was limited to the relative wealth and privilege of those in attendance—a feast that looked a lot like the one Jesus warned against in Luke 14:12-14.

Jesus' warning is against inviting friends, relatives, or "your rich neighbors" (v. 12) because they might invite you back—and in a culture built on reciprocity, the danger of inviting your friends was that you were not generously giving away your resources but bolstering your social status. Jesus' instructions to push back against a culture of power-mongering and status-seeking was to invite "the poor, the crippled, the lame, the blind" (v. 13) although they cannot repay you.

The same is true today: the spiritual discipline of feasting is not complete without constantly asking, "Who are we missing? Who are we not seeing because our position in society allows us to avoid them?" This will look different in different contexts, but at the very least it should involve asking ourselves if we have enough relationships with the poor that our offers of meals don't look like hollow charity but full-hearted celebration. It should involve asking ourselves questions about accessibility—do our churches and homes have the necessary means for the disabled and chronically ill to access them?

If the point of Jesus' admonition was to deconstruct social expectations about patronage and reciprocity, our feasting cannot be thinly veiled service work that treats the marginalized as projects we graciously condescend to. Our feasts as family should rather include the poor and marginalized as fully recognized members of our community worthy of celebration. Feasts were intended, similar to the way the sabbath year and Jubilee regulated land ownership and debt, to push back against our selfish bent toward hoarding resources.

In August of 2017, several Texas oil refineries shut down in anticipation of Hurricane Harvey hitting the southeast coast. Across the state, fearful drivers stocked up on gas in any way they could—filling their tanks, purchasing extra containers to fill, waiting in long lines. The resulting shortage led to many stations closing down for a few days that summer. In spite of multiple assurances that the refineries would be up and running quickly after the storm, people desperately hoarded resources out of fear. It's the same thing that happens when a snowstorm threatens to undo a community unaccustomed to cold weather: suddenly the grocery store shelves are stripped of bread and milk. While there is prudence in grabbing some essentials or filling up your tank before a storm, most people went beyond wisdom and hoarded resources—they took more than they needed, effectively taking from other people. When I buy four gallons of milk when I only need one, and the store runs out before the first snowflake falls, I'm taking milk away from someone else who needs it.

The rhythms of fasting and feasting are supposed to regulate these impulses—teaching us to sacrifice for the sake of others and give away our abundance to others. After all, what's the total opposite of hoarding resources? Extravagant giving. In other words, a feast.

There's no straight line between fasting and feasting and supporting the poor and marginalized politically. But there is a deep connection between practicing our biblical obligation to care for others and making that obligation such a deeply felt reality that it bleeds into our entire lives. When we understand that our consumption practices implicate others, we should find ourselves advocating for more responsible regulation of resources and more aid to the structurally disadvantaged. When we share meals and celebration with the marginalized, we gain a necessary political perspective, understanding more intimately the needs of others we would ordinarily avoid. The spiritual disciplines are always about the long game—bodily inhabiting big ideals, teaching our hearts and minds to want things we don't naturally want, and forming a community that witnesses to another kingdom. Perhaps our kitchens can be outposts of the kingdom of God, as well as our churches.

Hospitality

What comes to your mind when you think of hospitality? It might be the hospitality industry (hotels, resorts, etc.), or a friend or family member who likes hosting fancy events. Maybe it's the people in your life who regularly welcome you into their homes. Henri Nouwen noted that most of us think of hospitality as "tea parties, bland conversation, and a general atmosphere of coziness," and argues that if "there is any concept worth restoring to its original depth and evocative potential, it is the concept of hospitality."[9] Throughout church history, however, hospitality meant something much different: welcoming strangers and providing food and shelter for the marginalized or the foreigner. It was not about making a welcoming house; it was the moral foundation of all other good deeds: the second-century work *The Shepherd of Hermas* describes hospitality like this, in the middle of a long list of righteous deeds: "for the practice of hospitality results in doing good."[10]

Sharing meals and homes among believers is necessary and a beautiful representation of the kingdom, but practicing hospitality only directed toward friends and family misses a central part of the practice. In the early church, hospitality was practiced in such a radically countercultural way—crossing social and ethic divides by sharing homes and meals, which had great social significance—that Christian writers claimed that hospitality was itself evidence of the truthfulness of the gospel. In the fourth century, writers particularly focused on warnings against letting the practice devolve into a more culturally acceptable form, where hospitality was used to curry favor with the wealthy or powerful instead of welcoming the poor and marginalized.[11] Wealthy female Christians especially became examples of virtuous Christian hospitality. Where we have turned hospitality into a feminine virtue because we conceive of it as tastefully decorating a home and hosting an event well, early Christian women provided for people's needs in a deeply countercultural way.

It's not hard to see the political effects of this discipline—we are formed into a people who take seriously the biblical commands to care for the marginalized, even sacrificing our own comfort and security for their sake. We will surely make mistakes, a fear that often prevents Christians today from practicing hospitality. We fear not only our own safety or ease, we also fear offending foreigners with cultural insensitivities or the poor with social thoughtlessness. Catholic thinker and social activist Dorothy Day said of her own work, "Mistakes there were, there are, there will be. . . . The biggest mistake, sometimes, is to play things very safe in this life and end up being moral failures."[12]

The discipline of hospitality might be the greatest example of this idea I'm desperate to advance: our political beliefs and advocacy are not primarily built on grand, sweeping claims to which we mentally assent; they are often built on ordinary impulses and biases that we inherit and absorb in small, everyday actions. There's not a direct line between individual acts of hospitality and right political advocacy, but there is a meandering yet faithful line between our practices and corporate worship and moral formation that inevitably results in political action. Henri Nouwen said that in a society "increasingly full of fearful, defensive, aggressive people anxiously clinging to their property and inclined to look at their surrounding world with suspicion, always expecting an enemy to suddenly appear, intrude and do harm" that our vocation as believers is to convert "the enemy into a guest and to create the free and fearless space where brotherhood and sisterhood can be formed and fully experienced."[13]

Our acceptance of, service to, and celebration with those our society treats poorly should motivate our solidarity with marginalized communities in material—and this necessarily means political—ways. When we feel the dissonance between biblical mandates about caring for the poor and marginalized and the way our surrounding culture (including church culture) treats them, we will be prompted to action. This is why practices and disciplines matter—our bodily, experiential, habitual ways of learning to love our neighbors are more foundational and transformative than sermons about caring for the vulnerable. This should affect our stance toward the undocumented immigrant, the incarcerated, the disabled, the religious or racial minority, and the oppressed and marginalized.

This is the political community of the church's greatest identity: as receivers and givers of hospitality. "In other words, the church is called to participate in Jesus's hospitality among sinners and outcasts by embracing a stigmatized identity that follows from sharing life together with all of God's people."[14] The church needs to seriously consider why we've been so resistant and impervious to a stigmatized identity. What do we value more greatly than following God's commands? On the other hand, who would we need to invite to our table in order to truly have a stigmatized identity? That question might reveal more about who we are and what we are so resistant to than anything else.

The early church's focus on hospitality was inherited from Jewish understandings of hospitality associated with covenant and blessing—such as Abraham and Sarah and the three guests in Genesis 18, Rahab's hospitality of the Israelite spies, and the woman who invited Elisha in 1 Kings 17-18. The grand story of the Old Testament centers around God's relationship with his people—a hodgepodge of frequent foreigners who receive a promise that God will make them a people and give them a land. And this identity is intended to give them every possible reason to welcome foreigners themselves; because of their own relationship of dependence on God, they are commissioned to offer support to those who need it (Exodus 23:9). In the early church, this collided with ancient Roman culture and its economic structure of hierarchy and status. Patronage—an informal system of reciprocal favors or endowments—operated on the basis of social inequality. Where one person provided material or financial resources, the weaker party provided public acclamation or behavior that in some way bolstered the social status of the superior party.[15] "Central to the institution of patronage are reciprocity and competition,"[16] and so when resources are means of gaining social status or building up power, they become symbols of scarcity and conflict, opportunities to gain an upper hand on an opponent, not opportunities to bless a friend.

It is into this cultural and political setting barely dissimilar to our own that Jesus says that upon his return,

> the King will say to those on his right, "Come, you who are blessed by my Father; take your inheritance, the kingdom prepared for you since the creation of the world. For I was hungry and you gave me something to eat, I was thirsty and you gave me something to drink, I was a stranger and you invited me in, I needed clothes and you clothed me, I was sick and you looked after me, I was in prison and you came to visit me." Then the righteous will answer him, "Lord, when did we see you hungry and feed you, or thirsty and give you something to drink? When did we see you a stranger and invite you in, or needing clothes and clothe you? When did we see you sick or in prison and go to visit you?" The King will reply, "Truly I tell you, whatever you did for one of the least of these brothers and sisters of mine, you did for me." (Matthew 25:34-40)

This is the kind of hospitality we are called to practice: total abandonment of social status and hierarchy in the name of caring for others. When the epistles address hospitality (which they frequently do), the subject often addresses issues of social or economic inequality (Romans 12:13; Hebrews 13:2) and is seen as a requirement for leadership in the church (1 Timothy 3:2; Titus 1:8). Hospitality was not just about individual acts of charity but was about sustaining a community built on the early church's identity as foreigners who therefore treated the marginalized with care.

Part of what makes hospitality such a politically powerful practice is that it should break down our tightly held beliefs about the morality of poverty and wealth. When we are intentional about doing hospitality right—inviting the marginalized on the basis of equality (which requires that we accept hospitality *from* them as well)—we should be confronted with the illegitimacy of our assumptions about poverty. John Chrysostom, writing about hospitality, said that "even if you were positively certain that he were laden with countless iniquities, not even then would you have an excuse for depriving him of this day's sustenance. For you are the servant of Him Who said, 'You know not what spirit you are of.' You are servant to Him Who healed those that stoned Him, or rather Who was crucified for them."[17] If we are practicing hospitality within the institutional framework of the church, we should be in the constant process of ridding ourselves of the notion that poverty is immoral and that aiding the poor and marginalized requires they be properly "worthy."

Hospitality counterforms us against the prevailing political attitude of independence, reciprocity, and advantage-seeking. In a world that expects that people will fight for what they want, even at the expense of others, hospitality gives freely, taking on the risk of being taken advantage of for the sake of the other.

Theoretical desire for multiculturalism and mutual respect don't hold up under the weight of a complicated world—hospitality provides the tangible relationships and concrete social commitments required for true justice-seeking. Hospitality is nurtured not only by programs but by our worship that acknowledges our identity as foreigners and our dependence upon God, and as the telling and retelling of the stories of hospitality—in Scripture, in church history, and in our communities.

A Reminder

It's easy to read a chapter about spiritual disciplines and resolve to work harder at mastering them. You might pull out a calendar and plot all the disciplines you'll do in the next few weeks, call a friend and make an accountability pact, or simply put the book down with newfound resolve to try harder. But we ought to remember that we are not producing any effects ourselves by our efforts. The spiritual disciplines are not "spiritual" because they have no real effect on the material world; they are spiritual because they are means by which the Holy Spirit works in the life of the community of God.

The life of the church together pursuing Christlikeness in our inescapably political lives cannot be accomplished by sheer willpower. Just as we are powerless to save ourselves, we are powerless to produce spiritual growth in our own lives and the life of our community. C. S. Lewis said that when we practice "religious duties" we are "like people digging channels in a waterless land, in order that when at last the water comes, it may find them ready."[18] Practicing the spiritual disciplines prepares us for the work of the Holy Spirit. It's a little like learning a foreign language by living in another country—we place ourselves in the best possible place to learn, open ourselves up to learning the language through the help of others, and trust that our immersion will produce the knowledge in us.

9

A **Confessing City**

READING POLITICS WITH AUGUSTINE

Augustine was in a position to belittle the political culture of antiquity;
he could dismiss its achievements as "the fragile splendor of a glass
which one fears may shatter any moment"; he could do this without
turning his back on society as the Cynics did, simply because he
could point to a divine authority and a more lasting social order.

OLIVER O'DONOVAN

We cannot respond to the political disarray of our churches with didactic political education. The greatest tool the church has at its disposal is the methods that have sustained Christian life and practice for centuries: habits and practices, effectively communicated stories, and our lives lived together. And yet there is also a very real role for the church in providing political education—theological principles that guide not just our voting but our sober engagement in a dangerous political world.

There are no easy methods for this—no Sunday school curriculum, small groups, or reading plans. Every church in every tradition will have its own methods. Instead of prescribing a particular curriculum, I want to give one example of how we can learn to think about politics and "read" our political world, based in wisdom from one of the earliest and most influential Christian thinkers: St. Augustine of Hippo.

Augustine and Politics

I had a shaky introduction to Augustine. An early work of political theology I read in seminary was harshly critical of the African theologian
for his political pessimism and near-quietism. He believed, as most
patristic theologians did, that human government was instituted as a
form of remedial grace after the introduction of sin into the world. His
picture of the "two cities"—the earthly city and the city of God—seemed
to me to elevate the spiritual above the material and isolate Christians
in their own city, apart from the messy concerns of the earthly city suffering around them.

I was not wrong to find Augustine's political theology pessimistic—he
writes in *City of God* that no government can be truly just that does not
worship God, and his history of the Roman empire is full of evidence
that seeking earthly peace is pretty much futile. It is also really easy to
read his description of the earthly city as a description of earthly governments or nations instead of the way he intends it: the society of unbe-
lievers on earth, demons, and Satan. The earthly city is the community
of beings turned against God, united by their disordered love of themselves or material goods above God. The city of God is the society of
believers and angels, a community united by their love of God.

Most scholars agree that Augustine is politically pessimistic—and in
the context of his time, when other Christians were infatuated with
Constantine's conversion and the birth of Christendom, that was
probably a good thing. And yet there is another element to Augustine's
political theology: he was personally very politically engaged.[1] Through
his letters and sermons, we now know that Augustine pled with political
leaders against capital punishment, even on behalf of those who had
harmed the Christian church.[2] In his writings he is concerned about
disciplining the desires of citizens of earthly nations,[3] he commends
the public official Macedonius for his desire for the heavenly city,[4] and
he dedicates *City of God* to another public official, Marcellinus. His personal correspondence demonstrates that Augustine viewed the civic

duties of leaders as intimately connected with their citizenship in the city of God, not in competition with it.[5] The tension between Augustine's pessimism and activism produces a question relevant for all Christians struggling with politics: How can we have a pessimistic account of human political institutions—knowing that they are passing away and corrupted by sin—and yet still faithfully participate in politics? Or in Eric Gregory's words, "Can there be a kind of idealist disenchantment without political disengagement?"[6]

Confessions and *City of God*

Augustine's work on original sin and predestination has deeply shaped the Western church. He lived at a unique moment in Christian history, just at the beginning of Christendom. Augustine's two important works are probably *Confessions* and *City of God*, the first telling the story of his life and conversion, and the second a sprawling account of biblical and Roman history that responds to the claim that Christians were to blame for the fall of Rome. These two works are often interpreted and understood entirely differently—one as religious memoir and the other as pessimistic political theory. But a comparison between the two central works provide helpful principles for addressing the tension Augustine felt and that all Christians face: placing no hope in the political system for transformation even while faithfully seeking political change.

There are good reasons for comparing these two works. Augustine himself compares individual humans and their communities, just as many philosophers and thinkers before him. Just as Plato compares the right ordering of a human soul and the right ordering of a city, Augustine describes humans and cities as fundamentally analogous: both are ordered by their loves, both are tempted toward the *libido dominandi* (the desire to dominate),[7] and both find their ultimate happiness only in God.[8] Augustine does not craft an abstract theory of political structures but articulates his view of a world animated and limited by the capacities of the human soul.[9] His clear connection between the individual and the city requires that we understand *Confessions* and *City of*

God in light of one another: the history and guiding story of the divided cities and the history and guiding story of the divided self.

Principles for Positive Political Action

There's another important similarity between these two works: they are descriptions of deficient educations and blueprints for reeducation. In *Confessions*, Augustine analyzes the results of a deficient education for an individual, and in *City of God* he analyzes the results of a deficient education for a community. Both stories use history—of a person or of a community—and reinterpret that history in light of Scripture, undoing all the wrong lessons that Roman culture and civic education had instilled. They are, in different ways, catechetical texts—educating Christians about spirituality, philosophy, politics, and social life. Augustine's aim in both cases is to educate—to educate Christians about the false trappings of worldly success or persuasive philosophies in one work and to educate Christians to better recognize and avoid the temptations of empire in the other.

This makes these texts—and Augustine's life and teaching as a whole—especially instructive for Christian leaders and teachers desperate for new ways of thinking about Christian political witness. The following are three principles for creative political action that we can gain from Augustine. They are not methods for instruction or a curriculum to follow; rather, they are lenses for thinking about distinctively Christian political work and education. Most Christian leaders and educators should read both works, but even if they are new to you, these three principles should spark some ideas in the meantime about how to faithfully minister to people in an inescapably political world, in whatever capacity you find yourself.

Critique of perfection. One aspect of earthly political engagement that is so difficult to sustain for Christians awaiting the coming redemption of the world is its imperfect nature. Until Jesus returns, we are never finished working to steward this creation, and our efforts will always be tainted by sin and difficulty. Augustine is a theologian who was painfully aware of how imperfect all our efforts at political work would be. He was born a few decades after Roman emperor Constantine's conversion, and he witnessed the beginning of the end of the Roman empire toward the end of his life. He lived in a newly Christianized empire, in dialogue with theologians who held theocratic hopes of a new age of Christian rule on earth, and yet he also witnessed the fragility of this earthly institution.[10]

Both *Confessions* and *City of God* provide critiques of perfection in light of the coming kingdom of God;[11] both also dwell on the present "in-between time," a time of a will divided by desires for God and temptations toward material things, and a time of unfulfilled longings. These are stories of an individual who continues to battle sin even after his conversion, and of the pilgrim people of the church who continue to live in a broken world—and Augustine refuses to ascribe perfection as either the reality or the goal.

In *Confessions*, Augustine faces lingering temptations toward sexual immorality and pride. He remains reliant upon grace in the midst of his personal struggles, the story never shifting to one of triumphant personal victory. In *City of God*, the attitude is remarkably similar: while Augustine encourages Christian leaders to continue in their difficult political work, he remains unconvinced that this new development of Christians holding political office alters his pessimism about political work. This persistent denial of perfection does not necessarily seem to offer much in the way of resources for political action, but in reality it helps Christians achieve the creative thinking we need by freeing us from the constraints of pragmatism.

In books seven and nine of the *Confessions,* there are two stories of Augustine experiencing the presence of God—one appears to be a failure and the other a success. Yet theologian Charles T. Mathewes argues, the second instance is best understood as "equally a continuation of the same pattern of temporary intimacies, fleeting achievements."[12] In Augustine's own life, experiences with God are not definite events significant in themselves but are narrated as one moment in the larger story of a life, events that only gain their full meaning in the context of a larger narrative.[13] The interpretation of these moments is more important that the moments themselves, because their significance is found in the larger story they inhabit, not in the "success" or "failure" of the particular event.

Augustine does not determine the significance of an event based on its immediate success or failure but maintains that its significance is only found in eternity,[14] and this same attitude is a helpful way for Christians to learn to think about politics. A glimpse of God is good because of the place the experience occupies in a larger story of his providence and mercy, not because it meets some human evaluation of success in the moment. In this understanding of events—both personal and corporate—dissatisfaction is no longer evidence of failure but foretaste.

So, rather than operating within a success or failure mentality that constrains political activity along pragmatic lines, Christians have greater creative possibilities. Actions—political and otherwise—can take on significance based not on their own success but on the extent to which they align with the political community of the city of God. Questions about strategy are not obliterated, but they can no longer take prominence. Time and money spent working toward political measures seeking true human flourishing are never wasted, because expending them does not depend on humanly discernable success. The true significance of political work "will only be apprehensible for humans from the end of time, and not a moment before," says Mathewes.[15] This does not mean that present political work has no theological significance, but that Christians are freed from the constraints of merely "here and now" thinking.

City of God not only severely tempers our expectations for meaningful political work, it also provides a new measurement—rather than evaluating an action's immediate success, Augustine's work outlines the features of these two opposed communities as descriptions that help discern between different political actions. Does it align with the earthly city and her bent toward pride and domination, or does it align with the love of God and neighbor that characterizes the city of God, even if in the moment it "fails"? When political work is reflecting or pointing to another, greater reality, success is not measured against an ideal—how close you can get earthly political institutions to look like the city of God—but by how faithfully the work points to a reality only God can create.

Local political work with a small circle of impact, legislation that does not pass, court cases with odds stacked against the more righteous side, voting for or against a politician who will certainly win regardless of your vote or advocacy—these all gain their significance outside of their immediate results. Political work can be right and good without being successful or permanent, so Christians are freed from attachment to any particular political structure and flexible enough to remain faithful in whatever context or circumstances they find themselves.

Reading history—or not. A related resource that this comparison between *City of God* and *Confessions* provides is a right relationship to "reading" history. Many of us have been taught that one thing Christians must do in our political and cultural engagement is to "read the times," looking for clues in the headlines for theological significance or looking at the history behind us and seeing what it really means in light of the story of Scripture. And while *City of God* is a powerful example for Christian leaders of how to work at pulling back the curtain and exposing the true story of empires, it is also fundamentally uninterested in grand historical interpretation claims. The reason for this caution is found in a similar aversion in *Confessions*: the problem of autobiography. Both autobiography and historiography tell us a story about ourselves or our people, giving us an orientation to the world and an identity from which to operate. Yet both of these stories are slippery, heavily influenced by the biases of self-narration: we are always in the middle of the journey, disoriented because we cannot have a God-level perspective on our own experience.[16]

The problem of autobiography and historiography is the reason Augustine needs to couch both his own story and the story of the whole world in the context of the grand cosmic story of redemption revealed in Scripture, the only history or biography of which we can be certain.

Scripture is historical material with the kind of perspective humans are incapable of inhabiting. All history outside of Scripture is done without God's ultimate perspective on historical events to assess their meaning because the whole of human history is accessible.[17] This is why the narrative of the two cities is so important—we cannot judge the contours of our history accurately without God's perspective, but we can observe the contours of the two cities operating in history, animating the loves of particular nations or leaders. Augustine is happy to assign the actions of people and nations to the earthly city but not so eager to say exactly what these events mean.

This is best exemplified in his description of Roman history. Theologian Gregory Lee argues that by the time Augustine began writing *City of God*, he had seen enough political surprises that he was aware of the ambiguity of history and humanity's consistent failure to accurately assess the significance of contemporary events in God's redemptive plan.[18] Where some Christians saw Rome as God's "instrument of salvation" or "a satanic manifestation of the earthly city," Augustine saw Rome as we in our limited perspective must see all human institutions: as theologically ambiguous.[19] Once Rome was sacked, he again refused to argue as other Christian theologians were arguing, that this was a sign of the end times.[20] He recognized God's punishment of a sinful city but refused to give Rome's fall deep theological significance in light of the trajectory of all history.

Throughout Augustine's historical description of the two cities, there is remarkably little attempt to ascribe theological significance to specific events. Instead, it's backwards: the reality of the two cities is discerned from the inspired history of Scripture, and then history is interpreted in light of that division. Even in book one, as Augustine offers an explanation for why Christians and pagans alike suffered in the sack of Rome, and why suffering happens more generally to both the righteous and the unrighteous, he does not dwell on why those things happened but on how they affect the people of the two cities differently. Rather than confidently asserting why Rome was sacked—though he does not shy from calling it judgment[21]—the focus is on how the central division of humanity, the city of God and the earthly city, is evidenced in how members of those communities respond to suffering and difficulty.[22]

Once again, this does not initially appear to be much of a resource for political action but in fact forcefully opposes some of the most constraining tendencies in our political work today. Much theologically vacuous political work is grounded in a poor understanding of time and history: "This is the most important election in our lifetime!" is a prime example of the human tendency to take on God's perspective without warrant. Similar to the theologians bickering over different interpretations of Rome's role in the grand scheme of redemptive history, Christians are often tempted to ascribe deep theological significance to historical events.

President Trump has been credited as a modern-day Cyrus, decried as a harbinger of God's judgment on America, or held up as evidence of America's status as a favored nation. The 2016 election was filled with claims about how this moment in history was so significant, with such frightening potential consequences, that otherwise immoral or unwise decisions needed to be made. Some Christians saw in the potential for multiple Supreme Court justice nominations such a significant historical moment that Trump needed to be elected. Outlets from *The Hill* to the Billy Graham Evangelistic Association argued that this election was the most important one in our lifetime.[23] Regardless of the particulars, the prevailing narrative was the same: the significance of this moment in time should change your political and ethical calculations.

And just as Rome was the subject of decline narratives, communities throughout history have had their political work constrained by stories of immanent decline, a corruption of long-standing values, and fear of a changing future. Political scientist Andrew R. Murphy compares the rhetoric of Roman decline to New England Puritans interpreting crop failures as evidence of God's judgment on their community or the commentary by the likes of Pat Robertson and Jerry Falwell after 9/11 that blamed America's moral decline for the attacks.[24]

Augustine's historical narrative contradicts these tendencies: since we cannot read the historical progression of the world or ascribe particular theological significance to specific events, Christians can only evaluate the loves and trajectories of communities and institutions and make faithful decisions. This is a greater impetus for political work than an understanding of history that constrains our work to operating under faulty assumptions about who is playing what role and what "time" it is in the grand scheme of all history. All Christians can judge is the loves and loyalties at the heart of political decisions and not whether they are somehow justified or qualified by their place in history.

In the face of apocalyptic fear-mongering or grandiose assertions about the overriding importance of lesser-of-two-evils choices, this refusal to give weighty significance to historical events provides a more faithful, consistent, and God-dependent way of engaging politically. Because Christians cannot judge the significance of political events within the historical arc, every critique is flexible and ad hoc.[25] There are no eternal pronouncements against particular policies or systems unless based explicitly in Scripture, and there is freedom to work within a variety of structures and with people of various backgrounds and convictions.

Augustine's view on history allowed him to celebrate the work of Christian leaders when it aligned with the city of God and criticize when it did not. Augustine's praise of Theodosius in *City of God*, for example, is notably missing any description of glory or power but features actions and characteristics decidedly in opposition to or totally irrelevant to the efficient ordering of the empire.[26] He praises the leader for not clinging to his power, not being motivated by private grudges, and doing penance for his mistakes.[27] Rather than justifying his mistakes or qualifying his immorality because of his importance in history, Augustine was able to criticize and commend on the basis of the actions themselves.

Augustine does not find history meaningless or disconnected, as many of his pagan contemporaries did,[28] but was suspicious of human efforts to adequately discern the meaning of events. Augustine certainly understood God as working in history,[29] and he undoubtedly understood

Christians as having *some* ability to read the signs of the times, but his awareness of our limited perspective kept those other ideas from exerting undue influence on his political theology. He had a truly "political theology" as defined by Oliver O'Donovan: recognizing earthly events of liberation and justice as "partial indications of what God is doing in human history" while consistently looking not to our own history but to "the horizon of God's redemptive purposes" in order to truly understand the significance of political events here and now.[30] The closest we can get to "reading" history is recognizing these partial indications, events we only recognize by knowing how Scripture describes God's redemptive purposes.

Confession as political action. Another way Augustine provides helpful principles for pastors and teachers thinking about how to educate and form their communities in the political sphere is by thinking of political work as a form of confession. Augustine's seminal political work, *City of God*, is an example of political confession we can emulate in our teaching and living. It occupies the middle space between lament and hope, painfully aware of the limitations and deficiencies sin has placed on human action and yet directing human longing toward the source of ultimate redemption. Throughout the historical description of the two cities, there is both longing and lament: longing for a community of people rightly ordered by their love of God and lament over the evidence of corruption and pride in the earthly city. And yet, in the context of these particular, concrete communities and their histories, there is "occasional delightedly surprised recognition of the *vestigia*, the traces, of God's city,"[31] even in Babylon or Rome.

Confession as described by Augustine is never merely recognition of sin but includes corresponding praise: a recognition of how things are, a longing for how they should be, and a celebration of the hope that they one day will be made right. The city of God gives us a picture of eternal, perfect community that shapes our political identity.[32] As teachers and leaders, there are abundant opportunities to paint a picture of a social and political future that prompts lament over our current shortcomings and yet draws our desires toward a better community. How you paint that picture will look different in different contexts, but Augustine gives us a real-life example via his writings and sermons, and especially in *City of God*, as to how to educate people toward longing and not just give them information.

Political confession is not merely about acknowledging our wrongdoing but about renarrating our past and present in light of the truth of the gospel. In *Confessions*, Augustine renarrates his life story, a story that could be told by his unbelieving contemporaries as a story of glory and success but that he tells as a story of dissatisfaction and suffering.[33] Similarly, *City of God* renarrates the story of the Roman empire in opposition to the false stories of Roman civic virtue and pride. Like a "nineteenth-century free-thinker demolishing a religious belief,"[34] Augustine deconstructs the narratives that shaped Roman life. His meticulous dismantling of the stories Romans told themselves about their history and values did not serve merely to condemn their wrong worship or disprove their historical claims but to expose the story as artificially constructed.[35]

The stories we tell about ourselves and our histories matter. As we outlined in chapter one, the abortion myth is a powerful story we tell ourselves that paints our leaders in a better light than they deserve to be seen in: we ignore their support of segregation and the racial politics motivating evangelical engagement by telling a story that highlights the real concern for abortion at the expense of the more troubling parts of the story. The story we tell ourselves about our nation's supposedly Christian founding can justify the sins of our forefathers by emphasizing their Christian convictions and ignoring their racism. The beauty of political confession—of telling the truth about ourselves and our histories in light of Scripture—is that it reveals artificial stories for what they are and creates space for truer ones.

Confession—a practice that sounds suspiciously apolitical, erring on the side of Augustine's pessimism—is surprisingly capable of animating political activism. It recognizes human limitations and dependence on God, but it also illuminates false stories for what they are, centers laments and longings on the true story of cosmic redemption, and prevents political work from embodying undue confidence in particular structures or ideals.

Political Imagination

Augustine's theological depth and pastoral heart are what make his works so significant for pastors and leaders seeking to bring congregations through our complicated political times. He too faced the difficulty of an empire that was violent and immoral and yet claimed a Christian identity. He too faced the complications of offering pastoral wisdom to congregants tempted to rely upon the strength of an earthly empire for protection and provision. He too grappled with his pessimism over political possibilities and his desire to faithfully live in a political world. For Augustine, political activity is no longer worthless just because humanity's greatest longings are fulfilled elsewhere, for such longing "reorients our being in the world."[36] Augustine's vision for the pilgrim citizens of the city of God is communicated via a story, a grand, sweeping, historical narrative that orients them both within their own community and in relationship to the opposing one. They have greater freedom to cooperate with citizens of the earthly city because they know the stories that animate the two cities, and this knowledge fosters in them a strong sense of identity and a familiar wariness toward the competing stories they encounter.[37]

Both of these principles share a common characteristic: they release us from our captivity to political constraints and prompt us toward greater creativity. If there's anything that American evangelicals need more of, it might be creativity. We are so often constrained in our political thinking and decision making by forces that trick us into thinking that our options are severely limited and the consequences for working outside of them are great. We need our political imaginations enlarged to help us think outside of the constraints of pragmatism, our own historical moment, and the dominating stories of our earthly political communities. Each of these principles is based in nurturing our creativity and exposing the supposed limitations of our political thinking as false.

This is what will keep pessimism from leading to inaction: creative, imaginative thinking with an eschatological orientation. Augustine's theology, particularly the narrative of the two cities, properly understood in relationship to *Confessions*, helps pilgrim citizens of the city of God seek policy change and social transformation that is neither entirely hampered by theologically informed pessimism nor constrained by the competing stories of the earthly city.

Creation Redeemed

ESCHATOLOGY AND POLITICAL FORMATION

Revelation does not respond to the dominant ideology by
promoting Christian withdrawal into a sectarian enclave that leaves
the world to its judgement while consoling itself with millennial dreams.
Since this is the standard caricature of the apocalyptic mentality, it must be
strongly emphasized that it is the opposite of Revelation's outlook, which
is oriented to the coming of God's kingdom in the whole world and calls
Christians to active participation in this coming of the kingdom.

RICHARD BAUCKHAM

I grew up reading the Left Behind books (The Kids editions, actually). I had recurring nightmares about the series as a child, and while the particular fears of being abandoned on a postrapture earth faded as I grew up, the unease surrounding the last days or end times continued. I'm not the only one affected by the Left Behind books—Barna found in 2001 that 24 percent of American adults were aware of them (by comparison, 69 percent of American adults were aware of the Harry Potter books), and almost one out of every ten Americans had read at least one.[1] Similarly, Hal Lindsey's 1970 *The Late Great Planet Earth* contributed to one of the many eras of popular obsession with the end times that the United States has experienced—the book didn't make explicit predictions but strongly suggested that the rapture/ tribulation would happen in the 1980s.

While these books and their corresponding films, video games, and spin-offs were written in the 1970s to the 1990s, they contributed to the popular understanding of eschatology for entire generations of evangelicals. We grew up with the expectation that the end of the story was the destruction of creation after the plucking of the faithful from the earth— and that our lives should be lived in light of waiting for that promise.

Our popular language reveals how much we've been shaped by these expectations, even before the advent of Christian end-times fiction and fascination. "Going to heaven" permeates our language about the gospel and evangelism: we are often trained to ask people if they know "where they're going," and we imagine what it will be like "in heaven" when we talk about eternity. The evangelistic crusades of the twentieth century were populated by language about sending people to heaven— Billy Graham is said to have quipped, "My home is in heaven. I'm just traveling through this world." D. L. Moody said that he looked at the world "as a wrecked vessel. God has given me a lifeboat and said, 'Moody, save all you can.'" Similarly, the popular saying, "You don't polish the brass on a sinking ship," is often attributed to popular radio preacher J. Vernon McGee.

Why include a chapter on eschatology in a book about how our worship affects our politics? Our eschatology is not just incorrect if it ends in heaven, it has dangerous political and social effects on our world today—and the correction to that is right worship. The eschatology of the church has always been a theme of her worship, but the evangelical obsession with end-times predictions, charting out timelines, and focusing our attention on heaven keeps our worship and our eschatology separate—and that has disastrous political consequences.

If the church's eschatology is a cryptic academic exercise, it won't affect her daily life together and her work in her community. However, the orientation of all people, communities, and institutions is toward some end: we are living and working and creating toward a vision of where the world is headed. Dietrich Bonhoeffer said that the church "witnesses to the end of all things. It lives from the end, it thinks from the end, it acts from the end, it proclaims its message from the end."[2] The church, as a community of people who do not believe that reality is bound by what we see and hear around us, *especially* lives and proclaims its message from the position of the "end" we envision—but what end? What are the current consequences of an immaterial, disembodied, "floating in the clouds" vision of the end? And what are the current consequences of a material, redeemed vision of the end?

Why Eschatology Matters

I love church potlucks. There's community, a strange mix of food to satisfy anyone's cravings, and there's always leftovers. A friend of mine, Stephanie, always brings something delicious and beautiful: a perfectly iced three-layer chocolate cake, a dessert shaped like a football field during the national championship game, gorgeous rows of homemade cupcakes. I, on the other hand, usually forget that the potluck is happening and throw something together the morning of. I love cooking, but I tend to have a certain narrative going in the back of my mind: this is just going to get eaten, quickly, by people who don't know who made what. (Terrible, I know).

There's a world of difference between the work Stephanie puts into the food she brings and the work I put in. I think of my cooking as a means to an end, a creation that will be quickly devoured, a bump in the road on my way to the work I have to do at the start of the week. Stephanie knows that her work will bring people joy, that the effects of her work will last beyond their consumption, that the cooking is valuable work to enjoy. Our work on earth is changed—both in content and in motivation—by the end we have in mind. What will our work be used for? Will it be used at all?

Our politics, too, are shaped by our eschatology. Evangelicals have frequently connected our eschatology to our political activism: Our interpretations about specific prophecies have influenced support for

Israel. Hard-line Cold War policies were supported by connecting end-times prophecies to communism. A general disposition of apathy toward material suffering can be justified by appealing to a coming destruction of the earth. Our understanding of how to interpret end-times prophecies obviously impacts our understanding of international politics and developments in world history, but perhaps more than that, our general vision of the end of the story shapes our judgment of political goodness and our willingness to engage in political action.

"It's All Gonna Burn"

In his book *Surprised by Hope*, N. T. Wright notes that English evangelicals "gave up believing in the urgent imperative to improve society (such as we find with Wilberforce in the late eighteenth and early nineteenth centuries) about the same time that they gave up believing robustly in resurrection and settled for a disembodied heaven instead."[3] The same could be said of American evangelicals: our apathy surrounding political efforts to create flourishing in our communities is directly connected to how much our vision of the end includes a bodily resurrection and material redemption of creation. If "it's all gonna burn"—if the ship is sinking or is already wrecked—what's the point in working to create better material conditions for suffering people? You might as well take as many people in your lifeboat as you can, instead of trying to rearrange deck chairs on the *Titanic*.

But what if the ship isn't sinking? Or more accurately, what if it *is* sinking but isn't doomed to end up on the bottom of the ocean? The vision the Bible paints for the future of the world is just like that of our bodies: redeemed, made new, perfected—not destroyed and started all over again. The promise of redemption instead of destruction begins in the Noahic covenant in Genesis 9: after a flood has destroyed all life on earth outside of the safety of the ark, God makes a promise to Noah that "Never again will all life be destroyed by the waters of a flood; never again will there be a flood to destroy the earth" (v. 11). All the evil and wickedness on earth prompted God to essentially wipe the slate clean and start over, though with a family that will promptly exhibit that sin affects and infects all people.

This covenant, the one made with all humanity and creation, that God says he is "making between me and you and every living creature with you, a covenant for all generations to come" (v. 12) promises that he will never again destroy his creation. And it's not likely that God is just talking about a moratorium on large-scale floods either. If we are headed for annihilation, "the language of everlasting covenant rings hollow" and the rainbow becomes "a cruel reminder that destruction is coming."[4]

The story of the flood in Genesis 7-9 reminds me of the 2017 film *Mother!* by director Darren Aronofsky, a metaphorical look at death and resurrection from the perspective of a self-described atheist who has nevertheless been deeply influenced by religious subjects.[5] The film begins with a shot of generic fire and destruction, before recreating a house and a woman from the dust and decay. The woman lives in a secluded home with her poet husband and spends her days tiptoeing around his writer's block while restoring their dilapidated home. One night, a stranger shows up at their door and her husband is quickly convinced to host the visitor, against his wife's quietly voiced wishes to the contrary. From that point on, nothing much but destruction follows: their guest (clearly an Adam figure) and his wife, who arrives shortly thereafter, slowly take over and destroy the home until the couple break the most coveted possession of the poet husband (who represents God).

The biblical allusions in the film are overwhelming, and viewers have spent many hours and words dissecting them. The more interesting detail, however, is the sustained focus on the work the wife of the poet is doing—she's restoring a home that the viewer has already seen go up in flames and be resurrected, and her visitors ask her why she's so intent on fixing up an old house when she could just knock this one down and build a new one. Even more interesting is that Aronofsky is also the mind behind the 2014 film *Noah*. A filmmaker with one work on Noah under his belt created another look at the consequences of a God who, when confronted with the evil of his creation, throws up his hands and starts all over again. In these stories, God is powerless to prevent his beloved creatures from destroying themselves, so he must wipe them out to create again, with a clean slate. The intruding woman's question about starting over and building a new house sounds remarkably like the end-times fascination of evangelicalism: Why polish the brass on a sinking ship?

Creation Redeemed

Christians have often failed to trust in God's vision for redemption. We've used an escapist eschatology and verses like "the heavens will disappear with a roar; the elements will be destroyed by fire, and the earth and everything done in it will be laid bare" (2 Peter 3:10) to justify a callous approach to cultural and political issues—especially environmental concerns. If the house is going up in flames anyway, why spend time painting the baseboards or adjusting the decor?

Before we look at the grand sweep of scriptural witness to the redemption of all things, let's figure out what this section of 2 Peter 3 is actually saying. The whole letter is about the truthfulness of the gospel and the second coming of Christ. In the face of doubters who scoff at the hope that the church has in the return of her Lord, Peter cautions against false teachers and encourages the church to put their hope in Christ's return. Right before verses ten through thirteen, Peter reminds us that the scoffers who say "ever since our ancestors died, everything goes on as it has since the beginning of creation" (v. 4) are forgetting one important exception: the flood (vv. 6-7). If the coming destruction of the earth is anything like the flood, the destruction will not be total: Noah and his family and the animals are all saved, and the actual earth is still intact when the waters subside. The flood was a cleansing much like the "fire" that will "lay bare" the earth to God's judgment.

The whole of Scripture witnesses to this coming restoration, redemption, and transformation of this same material earth we live on today. Jesus promises the coming "renewal of all things" (Matthew 19:28)—not brand-new things. Acts 3:21 tells us that Jesus must remain in heaven "until the time comes for God to restore everything, as he promised long ago through his holy prophets." The promise for the fulfillment of all things is the unity of all things in heaven and on earth under Christ (Ephesians 1:9-10) and the end goal is reconciliation (Colossians 1:19-20), not destruction. Most important in this discussion, in Romans 8:18-25, the *creation* "waits in eager expectation" and has been "subjected to frustration" but with "the hope that the creation itself will be liberated from its bondage to decay and brought into the freedom and glory of the children of God" (vv. 19-21). The creation is "groaning" (v. 22) along with "we ourselves" who are groaning in our waiting for the redemption of our bodies (v. 23). Our hope is not in being liberated from materiality but from decay that our current experience of materiality entails—and this hope and waiting are shared by creation as a whole.

The early church didn't talk about going to heaven when you die, partially because they lived with much greater expectation of the near future return of Christ, but also because they were often living in material suffering. Their hope was not in an escape from the world but in the return of their king, who will make all things right, vindicating their faith, ridding the world of oppression and evil, and ushering in the full expression of the kingdom. Christians living with a lot of privilege and wealth are much more likely to picture a spiritual future instead of a rectifying of the wrongs they've experienced on earth.

A Return to the Beginning

Perhaps the greatest biblical reason to understand the end of the story as one of redemption and not one of destruction is by looking back to the beginning. The vision of creation in Genesis is one where humans are commissioned to work in a garden: cultivating, creating, and flourishing. In the first telling of the story, in Genesis 1, God says that this humanity is made in his image "so that they may rule over the fish in the sea and the birds in the sky, over the livestock and all the wild animals" (1:26). Clearly this "rule" is not one of sheer domination—at this point human technology has not progressed to the point where there is very much that humans can do against lions or whales.[6] The first humans are not plopped into a perfectly tended garden and told to hang out in pre-fall bliss; they are given a job to do, and that job is to rule and reign over the earth.

There's nothing in the creation story that leads us to believe that Adam and Eve are intended to live in an untouched garden forever. They are commissioned to take the raw materials and natural resources God has given them and use their authority to shape the world. The fall does not introduce work, and it does not introduce human authority—but it does corrupt those good gifts. We can presume that the intention was for Adam and Eve to create a kind of city from their surroundings, places of human culture and creativity. The cities that follow exhibit the corruption that has taken place: Cain's city (Genesis 4:17), the creation of Babel to thwart God's instructions, and the great empires of Assyria and Babylon that threaten destruction for their enemies. And yet the call on God's people to cultivate creation and bring flourishing to the material world does not disappear: it is beautifully echoed in Jeremiah 29, in the midst of the ultimate example of sin and corruption. Even in exile, the people of God are given the same instructions they were given in the garden: to create flourishing in the place they have been brought (vv. 4-7). Even in a world filled with despair and destruction, their commission has not changed.

One of the most beautiful renditions of this I can imagine is the 1953 short story "The Man Who Planted Trees," by the French writer Jean Giono, which was also made into a short film in 1987. It tells of a young man who meets a strange and isolated shepherd in a desolated area, not far from a few cities either abandoned or dark with suffering and cruelty. The man spends a couple days observing the strange habits of the shepherd: he tends to his sheep with care but is also meticulous about planting acorns in the wasteland. The shepherd carries an iron rod for a walking stick, a tool that brings to mind physical power and maybe even violence, but he uses it to dig into the hard ground and plant his carefully selected acorns.

The young man goes to war, grows into a much older man, but keeps going back to visit his strange shepherd friend and witnesses the incredible results of his "quiet, regular work"—an enormous span of oak trees that bring life and beauty to the previously merciless communities surrounding him. By the end of the story, the man has completely transformed the land he lives in—there is water, giggling children, and "the kind of labor that only hope can inspire."[7]

This single man—"one man, one body, one spirit" the narrator calls him, much like the church—is an apt illustration of the commission and possibility of the church in a fallen world, a church that knows what the end of the story looks like and strives to realize some portion of it here and now.

A New Jerusalem

The vision that is intended to animate the work of the church on earth today is strikingly similar to the one in "The Man Who Planted Trees": a flourishing city. Revelation 20 and 21 paint a picture of the new heaven and new earth (21:1); the descending of the Holy City, Jerusalem, from heaven (21:10); and the restoration of the conditions of Eden (22:1-5). Unlike the city of Babel, humans are not working by their own strength and authority to subvert God's commands, but God is graciously restoring human flourishing to a world groaning for her redemption. Richard Mouw, explaining how Isaiah pictures this future Jerusalem, says that the "contents of the City will be more akin to our present cultural patterns than is usually acknowledged in discussions of the afterlife."[8]

This reality should alter our social and political commitments today, because the works of flourishing and creativity we labor at today will be appropriately redeemed and perfected in eternity. We are not biding our time on earth, waiting to be snatched away to an immaterial eternity. We are working on earth with the knowledge that every true work of human flourishing, done in the name of Jesus and by the power of the Holy Spirit, is a preview of the day that God's good creation is redeemed. Our political commitments should be centered around the question of what kind of communities, families, institutions, and natural environment will exist in eternity, and how we can seek glimpses of them today. If our understanding of the end of the story is a world that will be destroyed so we can live immaterial lives in heaven, our political decisions have more to do with short-term stability for spiritual work. The vulnerable and marginalized are usually the greatest victims of our belief that the kingdom of God is an immaterial, disembodied reality, because we fail to prioritize the material conditions that affect them now.

This redeemed creation will surprise us, since we are so immersed in our social structures and economic systems that we can barely see outside of the world's valuation of work. Just as Jesus' words about the kingdom surprised the leaders in his context, we need constant reminders of how upside-down this kingdom is and will be in eternity. Awaiting the redemption of the world also means teaching our hearts and minds to resist the way the world values human work and training ourselves to see things through the lens of the coming redemption.

There's one last argument that must be addressed: proponents of a general apathy surrounding political work on earth often remind Christians that our "citizenship is in heaven" (Philippians 3:20). In the context of Paul's letter to the Philippians, this little phrase would not have given the early church the impression that their identity was not bound up in a material earth and work on it. Instead, they would have understand the language of citizenship in the context of Roman colonies, created by the emperor with the purpose of spreading Roman culture and reaping the benefits of the colonies' work for the sake of the entire empire. The goal of these colonies (Philippi being one of them) was not for the citizens to eventually return to their rightful homes but to remind them of the role in bringing Roman culture to Philippi.[9] The return of Christ they were awaiting was not a return that promised to snatch them up to return with him, but a return where their rightful "emperor" would ensure their full flourishing, whether they needed aid against their enemies, the righting of wrongs, or the restoration of their full goodness.[10]

Whereas the church has often responded to material suffering and social problems with spiritual answers, Karl Barth notes, "The Word became flesh (John 1:14) and not the other way around!"[11] The same could be said about the material reality of the New Jerusalem: it comes down to earth in material form, and not the other way around! Our material world doesn't disintegrate into a spiritual reality but is redeemed and perfected by the gracious work of God. This vision of the future helps us critique the present. If our hope is immaterial, we don't have the same robust vision of future flourishing against which to judge the current world and to root our resistance. Revelation is the end of the Bible, but it ends with the beginning: the beginning of the new world, the full manifestation of the kingdom, and heaven and earth redeemed and reconciled. That's the beginning that should nourish our political imaginations—not the image of disembodied souls floating on clouds.

Political Eschatology

All areas of Scripture—inspired and profitable for our formation—have something to say about the political lives of believers. However, the book of Revelation might be one of the most politically significant works in the canon. Most popular works on Revelation promise to unlock or decode this supposedly cryptic work. Most of us fall into one extreme or the other, treating the book as a strange tirade about a future reality that does not affect our lives today or as a collection of codes and clues to decipher—which, incidentally, usually end up applying to the particular political powers of the interpreter's day. A couple years ago, I was leading a weekly sixth-grade small group, and one of my girls brought a Bible open to Revelation, filling me and my coleader with dread. Talking about Revelation is hard enough, I thought. Talking about it with middle-schoolers sounded impossible. Yet our apprehensiveness surrounding the book is preventing many of our churches, small groups, and Sunday school classes from benefiting from the unique political vision of the book.

There is obviously much disagreement about Revelation—we fight about how to approach the book (historical, predictive, theopoetic), what the symbols mean (Who are the two witnesses?), and how to use it in church teaching and worship. While these disagreements are not insignificant, they often obscure some of the important themes we can agree on. Sometimes these debates become so complicated and off-putting to the average Christian that they avoid the book altogether or rely unquestioningly on a single "safe" interpretation. Whether the book deals with historical realities, future prophecies, or general truths about human society and culture, there are political and theological truths that surpass those differences.

Revelation is a book for the church—for the seven churches listed in chapters two and three but also for the universal church. It serves the renewing of our minds (Romans 12:2), redirecting our perspective away from that of Rome or Babylon or the American empire to a kingdom perspective. Instead of decoding all the clues, we are beckoned by Revelation to inhabit a new sense of reality, to question the vantage point from which we've evaluated the world and gain a new perspective from the Creator of the universe. Some looked at Rome and saw progress, wealth, and knowledge instead of the death and destruction that sustaining her glory required. We can look at our own country or community and see the narrative of progress and inherent goodness, or we can see that the cost of privilege for some is the exploitation of others—it all depends on our vantage point.[12] After all, that's what an "apocalyptic" is supposed to do.

The word we translate *revelation* in the title and throughout the book is the Greek word *apokálupsis*, which literally means "uncovering," "disclosure," and "revelation." It's where we get the word *apocalypse*. Apocalyptic literature exists in biblical and extrabiblical literature, and defining it can be a little tricky—it's another area of debate, but the gist of it is this: it's a genre of literature in which revelation is given by an "otherworldly being" to a human recipient, disclosing another reality that is temporal and spatial—that is, showing future eschatological salvation and the supernatural world.[13] The writer Flannery O'Connor may have incidentally given us one of the best descriptions of the genre. In order for a Christian novelist to communicate disturbing distortions in the world that most people accept as natural or inevitable, she said, "you have to make your vision apparent by shock—to the hard of hearing you shout, and for the blind you draw large and startling figures."[14] When your audience shares your moral vision and your vantage point on the world, you can speak to them plainly, but when you need to awaken them to realities they are ignorant of, you might need to shock them into awareness. Similarly, author David Dark calls apocalyptic—a genre he sees in many modern cultural artifacts, like *The Simpsons* and Radiohead—the "maddening corrective" to this kind of callousness: it "highlights, exposes, or lampoons the moral bankruptcy of our imaginations while teasing us toward a better way of looking at, and dwelling within, the world."[15]

A Resisting Community

The early church often faced persecution because of their refusal to participate in the emperor worship that defined the common life of the people in the Roman empire. The original readers of Revelation would have likely connected its language and themes with Daniel, another apocalyptic work written during the reign of an empire that exerted complete control over its people and demanded their allegiance and worship. Revelation operates for these persecuted churches in a way similar to how Daniel spoke into the exiled community of his time: it comforts, strengthens, and emboldens a community to resist the claims of their oppressors.

Revelation is fundamentally about political resistance against the dominating systems of empire. It questions the plausibility structure of the empire by questioning the boundaries of the world. Over and against the claims of the empire, Revelation insists that there is another reality behind world events and the rule of powerful people. Revelation is not about empire as a vague reality, nor is it against any and all human authority or government structures. No, Revelation encourages the community of God to resist the abuse of power, economic exploitation, and worship of human authority that characterizes many earthly governments. Instead, Revelation functions as a critique of oppressive secular power, especially power that demands worship and allegiance.[16]

"Empire" indicates abuse of political power that is given religious sanction—which makes Revelation a message American evangelical churches desperately need. The sacralization of the political is a reality parallel to developments in our churches: we've blurred the line between patriotism and faithful Christian practice, we've allowed church services to take on nationalistic dimensions, and we've elevated the nation to the level of loyalty the church alone should occupy.[17] In opposition to this past and present temptation for churches, Revelation offers a vision of an alternate community that resists takeover by the powers of empire. It energizes a people by reminding them of who they are, who their God is, and what kingdom determines the real boundaries of their lives.

Revelation describes a political situation remarkably like our own: the dominating powers of economic systems threaten to destroy the earth, and the people of God are called to resist participation, even when it costs them. The "second beast" in Revelation is defined by how it forces "all people, great and small, rich and poor, free and slave, to receive a mark on their right hands or on their foreheads, so that they could not buy or sell unless they had the mark, which is the name of the beast or the number of its name" (13:16-17). Participation in the economic system required idolatry—a sacrifice the church could not make (14:6-11). The community was called to resist the power of this system as well as attack its greatest power: its claims to inevitability. In the face of political questions that are easily addressed by claims to pragmatism and realism, the church has a calling to question, resist, and offer a vision of an alternate future. Revelation instructs the church to ignore the "common sense" of the world as a guiding principle for life.[18]

Lest we think that Revelation paints these communities as invincible bastions of resistance against the empire, chapters two and three remind us of the broken reality all churches both live in and emulate. In the face of persecution, these historical communities are revealed for what they are: "scattered, isolated, witnesses before the massive solidity of the idolatrous empire."[19] The two basic indictments of the churches are that they are involved in idolatry via eating idol-food (2:14-15, 20) and complacency, probably due to comfort or wealth (1:4-5; 3:1-3; 3:15-17). Both condemnations are apparently rooted in the churches' desire to blend in as productive and ordinary members of society, participating in the economic systems and emperor worship and enjoying the benefits of their position in society. It is not that the church must isolate from society in order to maintain their faith, but that if they are living comfortably in corrupt economic and political systems they are in grave spiritual danger.

But the churches in Smyrna and Philadelphia are commended for remaining in poverty and affliction, and neither church receives a call to repent. To Philadelphia, John says, "I know that you have little strength, yet you have kept my word and have not denied by name" (3:8). In a world obsessed with power and prestige, this church is praised for their perseverance and faith with little strength. The operating power in Revelation is the idolatrous wealth of the world (18:11-20): those selling gold and precious stones, those who will mourn the loss of "luxury and splendor" (v. 14) and who gained their wealth from Babylon, for "In one hour such great wealth has been brought to ruin!" (v. 17).

The purpose of these letters at the beginning of Revelation is to "comfort the afflicted (Smyrna, Philadelphia) and to afflict the comfortable (Sardis, Laodicea)."[20] It is also to set the stage for the real revelatory truth: it is not merely the faithful yet fallen work of these believers that will resist empire, it is ultimately the power of God that will destroy all forces of oppression and abuse. Worship of the true God is a form of political resistance, one that also prevents "movements of resistance to injustice and oppression from dangerously absolutizing themselves."[21] The failure of these churches is not the end of the story—Revelation critiques the churches for their failures yet offers a necessary reminder that the power of redemption comes not from them but from the real agent of change in the book: the Creator and redeemer of the world, Yahweh.

Redeeming Power

Revelation also offers a new vision for a church immersed in a culture of brute force and domination, a kind of power found in sacrifice for the sake of others. Jesus as the slaughtered lamb appears twenty-eight times in Revelation, and the first time occurs in chapter five, in the throne room, when John hears a mighty angel ask in a loud voice, "Who is worthy to break the seals and open the scroll?" (v. 2). John weeps because no one is worthy to open it or look inside. Then one of the elders says to him, "See, the Lion of the tribe of Judah, the Root of David, has triumphed. He is able to open the scroll and its seven seals." (5:5). This is where we expect a triumphant king, a victorious warrior, a depiction of power that looks like domination, violence, and vengeance. Instead John looks to where the elder tells him to look and sees "a Lamb, looking as if it had been slain, standing at the center of the throne, encircled by the four living creatures and the elders" (5:6). After a further description of the lamb, the surrounding creatures and elders sing "a new song":

> You are worthy to take the scroll
> and to open its seals,
> because you were slain,
> and with your blood you purchased for God
> persons from every tribe and language and people and nation.
> You have made them to be a kingdom and priests to serve
>   our God,
> and they will reign on the earth. (Revelation 5:9-10)

The remarkable result of this display of power through sacrifice is a new people made up of every tribe and language and people and nation,

empowered to reign on earth as the kingdom of God. When the plausibility structure of the surrounding world narrows down our conceivable
options for the future into eat or be eaten, defeat or be defeated, rule or
be ruled, Revelation turns the regular categories of power on their heads
and declares that all humans were made to rule, to creatively assert
their God-given authority on earth.

The shock of this reversal of expectations awakens the community
to an important reality: God does not defeat the powers of sin and
darkness by human understandings of power or victory, but by self-
sacrifice and suffering. Similarly, in Revelation 19, the climax of the
mounting battle imagery, the heavenly warrior defeats the beast,
wearing a robe dipped in blood (v. 13). That's not a surprising image
unless you realize that the battle hasn't begun yet—the blood is his own.
Worshiping the God who begins a battle with his own sacrifice and wins
victory for his people through his own sacrifice makes it impossible to
justify our own abuses of power, our own overreach of authority, our
own malicious victories. We are not a team seeking to beat the other
team through domination, but a people defined by a slaughtered lamb.

Forming Our Eschatological Orientation

Revelation is a gift to a church surrounded by economic exploitation,
political idolatry, and abusive powers—whether it's the seven churches
in Revelation chapters two and three or the American church today.
Theologian Richard Bauckham says that one of the purposes of Revelation is to "purge and refurbish the Christian imagination." It is about
addressing the way that a dominant culture constructs the world and
challenging those assumptions by unmasking them for what they are:
a particular narrative upheld by the privileged for the sake of maintaining their power. Revelation should challenge believers today to
question power relations that seem inevitable, systems that we take for
granted, and "common sense" determined by the powerful.[22]

I don't want to offer highly specific instructions or examples for
churches to follow in achieving this—that will depend on your particular

context and needs. But there are a few nudges I can offer in the right direction, toward using Revelation in our worship and teaching, evaluating our eschatological orientation, and seeking the realignment of our practices with the coming kingdom.

Perhaps one of the most important ways we can integrate a better eschatology into our worship and practice is by listening to marginalized communities. Hopefully you've noticed how much of the preceding description of Revelation couched the church in terms of its marginalized position and minority identity. In some places and contexts today, the church still very much occupies this position, but this is not true for many American churches. Our understandings of Revelation must be informed by marginalized communities. A theology born out of resistance to political authorities from an oppressed position cannot result in private piety and political quietism unless it is read and practiced by the privileged. The most powerful readings of Revelation will always come from marginalized communities or those actively involved in opposition to unjust political systems. Some examples include Martin Luther King Jr., "Letter from Birmingham Jail"; civil rights activist William Stringfellow, *An Ethic for Christians and Other Aliens in a Strange Land*; and South African politician and cleric Allan Boesak, *Comfort and Protest: The Apocalypse of John from a South African Perspective*.

One everyday way our churches can resist the poor eschatology that prompts political apathy is by rejecting the material/spiritual dualism at every turn. As N. T. Wright explains, "The belief that heaven and earth could and sometimes did overlap and interlock is built into the very structure of ancient Israelite life, thought, and particularly worship."[23] Our worship could stand to look more like this recognition that the spiritual and material are integrated. Our answers to pain and suffering in sermons, songs, and counsel cannot promise a future escape for believers but must reassert redemption of all creation. Like many popular theological missteps that pastors or leaders would not affirm but that permeate our churches, for example, we could begin with a focus on our worship music. How often do our songs call heaven our home, encourage us to await heaven, or place all our future hope in a vaguely immaterial future? We can intentionally choose to worship with lyrics that celebrate the coming resurrection of our bodies and the redemption of the world.

James K. A. Smith says that Christian worship should give us a kind of inertia that is politically important, because we know that we are not sustained by political victory or social change but by the promises and faithfulness of God. "Lift up your hearts!" is a political admonition we hear every week.[24] Worship like this is a prominent theme in Revelation, depicting worship as the source of our resistance to idolatry and foretaste of the worship of the whole creation. God's kingdom has already come because there is a people who worship the rightful ruler.

The church's position as an eschatological community necessarily makes the church a "diacritical community."[25] Instead of merely criticizing the current age, we also call attention to the alternative. This is crucial because it retains the church's function in both supporting earthly government as authorized by God while criticizing the corruption and abuses of power that plague this age. As a witness to the coming kingdom of God, there is no government system, leader, economic program, or justice system that the church can support without reservation. We know that perfection awaits us. While we must support the best available options, making judgments about what systems and legislative options look most like the redemption we know we are awaiting, the church must also be constantly prepared to call out the abuses of even the systems it judges to be the best available options.

The way Christians change the world in Revelation is by worshiping God and trusting in his power and bearing witness to the kingdom. It's not by accumulating power at all costs or sacrificing convictions for the sake of particular hot-button issues, but it's also not by retreating from public life and the pressures of oppressive human authority. Instead, the church performs ongoing apocalyptic work: revealing the temporality and fragility of seemingly all-powerful authorities by worshiping the truly omnipotent God. We live in the tension between the future and the present, witnessing to the coming age while retaining a prophetic presence in the present.

Shalom

We began this book with a plea for spiritual formation in a political direction, and there's a reason for that: we are moving toward a political reality, and our formation should be in line with that reality. We can be formed toward any number of political realities, or we can be formed toward the ultimate political reality: the kingdom of God. Jesus' life was the embodied, holistic representation of that kingdom for us, constantly pointing his followers toward the healing, justice, and wholeness that characterizes it—*shalom*.

In our frustration and doubt over political realities, that word can be our guiding light. To translate *shalom* as "peace" is to flatten its depth and significance. In reality, shalom means something more like "wholeness," "intactness," or as I like to define it, "the way things are supposed to be." The healing, justice, and wholeness that Jesus embodied and freely gave—that's shalom. It's not absence of conflict or maintaining the status quo; it's the perfect flourishing of creation. We can mix up those two ideas, especially when it comes to our political activism.

A passage from Jeremiah perfectly illustrates how we should and shouldn't seek the shalom of our communities. In chapter thirty-eight, a few prominent men hear Jeremiah's proclamation—that the people need to leave the city and give themselves over to the Babylonians—and declare him a traitor. They go to the king and demand his death, because he is "discouraging the soldiers who are left in this city, as well as all the people, by the things he is saying to them. This man is not seeking the good of these people but their ruin" (v. 4). So they put him in a cistern to die. The king ultimately changes his mind and allows Jeremiah to escape the death awaiting him, but the accusation of the leaders hangs over his ministry: this man is not seeking the good (the shalom!) of these people but their ruin.

The irony is thick: the men accusing Jeremiah of treason are actually upholding a system that will cause the demise of their entire community. They think they are working for shalom, but it's the empty, status-quo version. Several chapters earlier, Jeremiah told the people God's promise for their shalom: to give themselves over to the Babylonians and in their captivity to settle down, build houses, plant gardens, make families, and seek the shalom of the city of their captors (29:5-7). Here is a strange vision of shalom: a vision in which there is life and creation in the midst of captivity and oppression. Jeremiah's plea for the people is to enjoy the real shalom of wholeness and healing that God promises if they will only obey him.

The evangelical church has a lot to learn from Jeremiah about political engagement. When we are faced with compelling evidence that our churches are captive to political forces, when our leaders dig in their heels and insist that nothing is wrong, when it looks like the people we love are forsaking their faith for temporal gains, this is the truth: sometimes, what looks like our destruction is actually for our good. I don't really blame anyone who thought Jeremiah was seeking their ruin when they saw him running around the city telling people that they would die if they stood their ground. I don't really blame anyone who called him a traitor when they heard his command to give themselves over to their idol-worshiping enemies. I don't really blame anyone who wants to listen to the voices that say that surely God wouldn't let this judgment come, not in this way.

There might be nothing more important for our ears to hear right now than the truth that our destruction might be for our good. Some of us feel like running through the streets screaming, "The Babylonians are coming! And we deserve it!" Others just see destruction that needs to be eased. It looks like our leaders, institutions, churches, and culture are being destroyed—and some of them are. We are witnessing idols smashed, broken systems exposed, evil theologies shattered. It looks like destruction because some of it is. It's tempting to find the people saying, "It's all going to be okay. Nothing really needs to change. A few tweaks maybe, but this city will stand, and we will protect it. God wouldn't let this judgment come, not in this way."

But there are consequences for our sin—including our institutional, generational, systemic, and corporate sin. Accepting those consequences can look as absurd as telling the people to stop fighting and give themselves over to their captors, but there are things that need to die:

Our attachment to a political party that knows it is the beneficiary of a lopsided bargain.

Deep-seated racism and misogyny that we like to imagine is behind us.

Institutional structures that protect the powerful instead of the most vulnerable.

Our impulse to fortify our own kingdoms.

We are living in a tumultuous time, and it can be hard to see how this chaos could be used for good. But refining requires fire, and rebuilding requires a little demolition. I think Walter Brueggemann said it best: "It is my judgment that the great pastoral opportunity among us is to utter faithful folk into the abyss too long denied, and to utter faithful folk through the abyss to newness, a difficult move given the despair among us."[1] No one wants destruction. And yet God often seems to work in this way: taking away the things we think we ought to love the most to make room for the newness He is in the business of constantly creating. Let's not cling to broken buildings and rotting kingdoms when the promise of redemption *then* is the promise of redemption *now*: he is building something better.

Acknowledgments

I suppose every author feels that their book is a snapshot of one period of their life—the things they were learning, the books they were reading, the people that influenced them—but surely this must be truer for a seminary student. This book is not my own; it is the product of every class I took, every book I read, every professor who challenged and instructed me, and every paper I wrote at Dallas Theological Seminary.

I want to especially thank Dr. Sandra Glahn, for telling me that if I waited until I was 100 percent ready, I'd never write it; and Dr. Barry Jones, for telling me to trust my voice and for three years of spiritual formation classes that changed my life. I also want to thank the professors whose classes especially affected this work: Dr. Glenn Kreider, Dr. Daniel Hill, and Dr. Michael Svigel. Thank you for teaching the kind of classes that challenged me, excited me, and allowed me to research what I love. Dr. Dorian Coover-Cox certainly deserves thanks, as well, for teaching me that procrastination is nothing but waiting until the building is on fire to walk the tightrope. There are so many people at DTS that helped me walk the tightrope—to face fear and write anyway—and I am deeply grateful.

The year before I started seminary, I took a writing class in college. I wasn't an English major, but in the midst of spiritual and political turmoil at Liberty University, I wanted to get to know Dr. Karen Swallow Prior. She sent my very first pitch to an editor, but I am mostly thankful for the days of peer editing in class when she encouraged and challenged me.

There have also been a host of people who have supported me through the actual writing process. Thank you Andrea Humphries for being my "internet big sister" who has not been afraid to give me a talking-to. Thank you Kat Armstrong for giving more than lip service to women seminary students. You're the real deal. Thank you Christ and Pop Culture writers, editors, and members—our little corner of the internet has changed me for the better. Thank you Katelyn Beaty for sending an email that changed my life. Thank you Ethan McCarthy and the rest of the IVP team for stewarding this work with me.

Thank you, lastly, to my family: my earthly family and my church family. Thank you Nana and Papa, Grandma and Grandpa, aunts and uncles and cousins. I am who I am because of my family, and I am especially thankful for the legacy of faithful Christ followers I was blessed to inherit. Thank you Grace Bible Church family, especially my Young Adult women. This is a book I wrote because I actually believe God has tasked the church with witnessing to his coming kingdom, and I am thankful beyond words that you trust me to help lead us in that work.

Notes

1. Apolitical or Unexamined

[1]While some decried the ruling (*Christianity Today* called it "counter to the moral teachings of Christianity"), most evangelical pastors and leaders said nothing about it, and many spoke of it positively. W. Barry Garrett of the Baptist Press said that "human equality and justice are advanced by the Supreme Court abortion decision." The 1971 Southern Baptist Convention annual meeting adopted a resolution that called on Southern Baptists to advocate for the legality of abortions in cases of rape, incest, severe fetal deformity, and mental or physical damage to the mother. W. A. Criswell, former SBC president and pastor of First Baptist Church in Dallas, said that he felt "it was only after a child was born and had a life separate from its mother that it became an individual person." From Randall Balmer, *Thy Kingdom Come: How the Religious Right Distorts the Faith and Threatens America, An Evangelical's Lament* (New York: Basic, 2006), 11-13.

[2]Joseph Watras and Mark B. Ginsburg, *Politics, Race, and Schools: Racial Integration, 1954-1994* (New York: Taylor and Francis, 1997), 55.

[3]William Martin, *With God on Our Side: The Rise of the Religious Right in America* (New York: Broadway Books, 1996), 173.

[4]Benjamin T. Lynerd, *Republican Theology: The Civil Religion of American Evangelicals* (New York: Oxford, 2014), 183.

[5]Lynerd, *Republican Theology*, 188.

[6]Kevin M. Kruse, *One Nation Under God: How Corporate America Invented Christian America* (New York: Basic Books, 2015), 277.

[7]Frances Fitzgerald, *The Evangelicals: The Struggle to Shape America* (New York: Simon & Schuster, 2017), 292.

[8]Jemar Tisby and Tyler Burns, "Interview: Andy Crouch," *Pass The Mic* podcast, January 3, 2017, player.fm/series/pass-the-mic-2440864/interview-andy-crouch.

[9]Lysa TerKeurst, Instagram, October 26, 2017, www.instagram.com/p/BauLfcUHlet/.

[10]James K. A. Smith, *Desiring the Kingdom: Worship, Worldview, and Cultural Formation* (Grand Rapids, MI: Baker Academic, 2009), 77.

[11]James K. A. Smith, *Imagining the Kingdom: How Worship Works* (Grand Rapids, MI: Baker Academic, 2013), 44.

[12]Rosalind Picard, *Affective Computing* (Cambridge, MA: MIT Press, 2000), 222.

[13]David Sax, *The Revenge of Analog: Real Things and Why They Matter* (New York: PublicAffairs, 2016), 238.

[14]Sax, *Revenge of Analog*, 238.

[15]"How Liturgical Are Today's Christians?" Barna, February 13, 2018, www .barna.com/research/liturgical-todays-christians/.

[16]For one example of a pastor witnessing this trend: Winfield Bevins, *Ever Ancient Ever New: The Allure of Liturgy for a New Generation* (Grand Rapids, MI: Zondervan, 2019), 18. This phenomenon, of younger Christians being drawn to older traditions, isn't entirely new either. In 1985, Robert Webber's book *Evangelicals on the Canterbury Trail: Why Evangelicals Are Attracted to the Liturgical Church* explored the theologian's own journey to the Episcopal church, and his subsequent books in the Ancient-Future series would describe ways that historic liturgies and practices of the church should impact the church's worship, evangelism, and service in the world.

[17]Todd D. Hunter, *The Accidental Anglican: The Surprising Appeal of the Liturgical Church* (Downers Grove, IL: InterVarsity Press, 2010), 14.

2. The Liturgy of Politics

[1]As we'll discuss later, it's not that we are unable to formulate penultimate beliefs—opinions about the best possible economic philosophy or system of representation—without fully accepting the ultimate beliefs of those we agree with or learn from, but that the force of those ultimate beliefs is always present and must be acknowledged and addressed.

[2]James K. A. Smith, *Awaiting the King: Reforming Public Theology* (Grand Rapids, MI: Baker Academic), 22.

[3]Smith, *Awaiting the King*, 21.

[4]James K. A. Smith, *Desiring the Kingdom: Worship, Worldview, and Cultural Formation* (Grand Rapids, MI: Baker Academic, 2009), 86.

[5]Robert E. Webber and Rodney Clapp, *People of the Truth: The Power of the Worshipping Community in the Modern World* (Eugene, OR: Wipf and Stock, 1988), 12.

[6]*On the Basis of Sex*, directed by Mimi Leder (Glendale, CA: Dreamworks, 2018).

[7]Christena Cleveland, *Disunity in Christ: Uncovering the Hidden Forces That Keep Us Apart* (Downers Grove, IL: InterVarsity Press, 2013), 45.

[8]This paragraph is lightly adapted from Kaitlyn Schiess, "No, This Isn't the 'Most Important Election in Our Lifetime,'" *Christ and Pop Culture*, October 19, 2016, http://christandpopculture.com/no-isnt-important-election-lifetime.

[9]Smith, *Desiring the Kingdom*, 54.

[10]Martha C. Nussbaum, *The Monarchy of Fear: A Philosopher Looks at Our Political Crisis* (New York: Simon and Shuster, 2018), 29.

[11]Molly Ball, "Donald Trump and the Politics of Fear," *The Atlantic*, September 2, 2016, www.theatlantic.com/politics/archive/2016/09/donald-trump-and-the-politics-of-fear/498116/.

[12]Ball, "Donald Trump and the Politics of Fear."

[13]Ball, "Donald Trump and the Politics of Fear."

[14]For more on the rise of the Religious Right, especially on this dynamic of alignment with the Republican Party, the addition of particular social and economic principles as inherently "Christian," and the concessions that became core doctrines, these titles will prove useful: William Martin, *With God on Our Side: The Rise of the Religious Right in America* (New York: Broadway, 1996); Randall Balmer, *Thy Kingdom Come: How the Religious Right Distorts the Faith and Threatens America, An Evangelical's Lament* (New York: Basic, 2006); Benjamin T. Lynerd, *Republican Theology: The Civil Religion of American Evangelicals* (New York: Oxford, 2014); and Kevin M. Kruse, *One Nation Under God: How Corporate America Invented Christian America* (New York: Basic Books, 2015).

[15]Bob Goudzwaard, Mark Vander Vennen, and David Van Heemst, *Hope in Troubled Times: A New Vision for Confronting Global Crises* (Grand Rapids, MI: Baker, 2007), 110.

[16]Smith, *Desiring the Kingdom*, 25.

3. Of This World

[1]Kate Bowler, "Death, the Prosperity Gospel and Me," *New York Times*, February 13, 2016, www.nytimes.com/2016/02/14/opinion/sunday/death-the-prosperity-gospel-and-me.html.

[2]Roland Marchand, *Advertising the American Dream: Making Way for Modernity, 1920-1940* (Berkeley: University of California Press, 1985), 24.

[3]Marchand, *Advertising the American Dream*, 206.

[4]Kate Bowler, *Blessed: A History of the American Prosperity Gospel* (Oxford: Oxford University Press, 2018), 226.

[5]Lisa Sharon Harper and David Innes, "Is the American Dream God's Dream?," *HuffPost*, October 31, 2011, www.huffpost.com/entry/christian-views-on-social-issues-american-dream-god_b_1035771.

[6]For reference, see Dominique DuBois Gilliard, *Rethinking Incarceration: Advocating for Justice That Restores* (Downers Grove, IL: InterVarsity Press, 2018); Peter Edelman, *Not a Crime to be Poor: The Criminalization of Poverty in America* (New York: The New Press, 2017).

[7]Chris Lehmann, *The Money Cult: Capitalism, Christianity, and the Unmaking of the American Dream* (Brooklyn, NY: Melville House, 2016), xiii.

[8]Lehmann, *Money Cult*, xxiii.

[9]This paragraph is adapted from Kaitlyn Schiess, "Patriotism or National Idolatry? Rightly Ordering Love of Country," CRI, www.equip.org/article /patriotism-national-idolatry-rightly-ordering-love-country.

[10]See Kevin Kruse, *One Nation Under God: How Corporate America Invented Christian America* (New York: Basic Books, 2015), 110: "While the passage of legislation amending the pledge to include mention of God was the result of pressure from Christian libertarian groups fighting against the New Deal, the popularity of a sermon given by Revered George M. Docherty of New York Avenue Presbyterian Church ('the church of the presidents'), and the resulting pressure to include God in political life, the desire for solidarity against communism became a vocal reason."

[11]Mark Noll, *One Nation Under God? Christian Faith and Political Action in America* (New York: Harper & Row, 1988), 9.

[12]David Dark, *The Gospel According to America: A Meditation on a God-blessed, Christ-haunted Idea* (Louisville, KY: Westminster John Knox Press, 2005), 9.

[13]Dark, *Gospel According to America*, 8.

[14]John Gramlich, "5 Facts about Crime in the U.S.," Factank, Pew Research Center, October 17, 2019, www.pewresearch.org/fact-tank/2019/01/03/5 -facts-about-crime-in-the-u-s/.

[15]Sarah Koenig, "A Bar Fight Walks into the Justice Center," *Serial* season 3, podcast audio, September 20, 2018, serialpodcast.org/season-three/1 /a-bar-fight-walks-into-the-justice-center.

[16]Quoted in Robert Wicks, *Touching the Holy: Ordinariness, Self-Esteem, and Friendship* (Notre Dame, IN: Ave Maria Press, 2007), 119.

[17]Lucia Zedner, "The Pursuit of Security," in *Crime, Risk, and Insecurity: Law and Order in Everyday Life and Political Discourse*, edited by Tim Hope and Richard Sparks (Abingdon, UK: Routledge, 2012), 202.

[18]Zedner, "Pursuit of Security," 210.

[19]Zoe Romanowsky, "Audrey Assad: American Daughter of a Refugee," *Aleteia*, June 23, 2016, https://aleteia.org/2016/06/23/being-the-daughter-of-a -syrian-refugee-has-shaped-audrey-assads-music-and-life/.

[20]Michelle Alexander, *The New Jim Crow: Mass Incarceration in the Age of Color Blindness* (New York: The New Press, 2012), 112. The 2010 Fair Sentencing Act reduced the disparity between these sentencing laws.

[21]Alexander, *New Jim Crow*, 113.

[22]Andy Crouch, *Strong and Weak: Embracing a Life of Love, Risk and True Flourishing* (Downers Grove, IL: InterVarsity Press), 35.

[23]Crouch, *Strong and Weak*, 40.

[24]Crouch, *Strong and Weak*, 104.

[25]Jemar Tisby, *The Color of Compromise: The Truth about the American Church's Complicity in Racism* (Grand Rapids, MI: Zondervan, 2019), 16.

[26]Brian Bantum, *Redeeming Mulatto: A Theology of Race and Christian Hybridity* (Waco, TX: Baylor University Press, 2010), 35.

[27]Bantum, *Redeeming Mulatto*, 36.

[28]Bantum, *Redeeming Mulatto*, 17.

[29]For more on a definition of racism, see Willie James Jennings, *The Christian Imagination: Theology and the Origins of Race* (New Haven, CT: Yale University Press, 2010) and Christopher S. Collins and Alexander Jun, *White Out: Understanding White Privilege and Dominance in the Modern Age* (New York: Peter Lang, 2017).

[30]Beverly Daniel Tatum, *Why Are All the Black Kids Sitting Together in the Cafeteria: And Other Conversations About Race* (New York: Basic Books, 2017), 8.

[31]Tatum, *Why Are All the Black Kids*, 188-89.

[32]Michael O. Emerson and Christian Smith, *Divided by Faith: Evangelical Religion and the Problem of Race in America* (New York: Oxford, 2000), 1.

4. For the Life of the World

[1]Barry Jones, *Dwell: Life with God for the World* (Downers Grove, IL: InterVarsity Press, 2014), 22.

[2]David P. Gushee, "Spiritual Formation and the Sanctity of Life," in *Life in the Spirit: Spiritual Formation in Theological Perspective*, ed. Jeffrey P. Greenman and George Kalantzis (Downers Grove, IL: InterVarsity Press, 2010), 213.

[3]Aaron Chalmers, "The Importance of the Noahic Covenant to Biblical Theology," *Tyndale Bulletin* 60, no. 2 (2009): 212.

[4]Christopher J. H. Wright, *Old Testament Ethics for the People of God* (Downers Grove, IL: InterVarsity Press, 2004), 212.

[5]Walter Brueggemann, *Old Testament Theology: An Introduction* (Nashville: Abingdon Press, 2008), 199.

[6]Stanley Hauerwas, *Approaching the End: Eschatological Reflections on Church, Politics, and Life* (Grand Rapids, MI: Eerdmans, 2013), 54.

[7]*The Epistle to Diognetus.*

[8]Gerald L. Sittser, *Water from a Deep Well: Christian Spirituality from Early Martyrs to Modern Missionaries* (Downers Grove, IL: InterVarsity Press, 2013), 53.

[9]Athenagoras, *The Plea for Christians*, XI.

[10]Kyle David Bennett, *Practices of Love: Spiritual Disciplines for the Life of the World* (Grand Rapids, MI: Brazos, 2017), xv.

[11]Robin Routledge, *Old Testament Theology: A Thematic Approach* (Downers Grove, IL: InterVarsity Press, 2013), 140.

[12]J. Richard Middleton, *The Liberating Image: The Imago Dei in Genesis 1* (Grand Rapids, MI: Brazos, 2005), 205.

[13]James Skillen, *The Good of Politics: A Biblical, Historical, and Contemporary Introduction* (Grand Rapids, MI: Baker, 2014), 11.

[14]For more resources on the nature of Christian political work, see James Skillen, *The Good of Politics*; Jonathan Leeman, *Political Church: The Local Assembly as Embassy of Christ's Rule* (Downers Grove, IL: InterVarsity Press, 2016); Charles T. Mathewes, *A Theology of Public Life* (New York: Cambridge University Press, 2007); and Oliver O'Donovan, *Desire of the Nations: Rediscovering the Roots of Political Theology* (Cambridge: Cambridge University Press, 1999).

[15]As Walter Brueggemann puts it, "What astonishes us and warrants our attention is that on occasion the affront against Yahweh is not a direct mocking of Yahweh or an abuse of Israel, but abuse of a third people that has nothing to do with Israel but, as it turns out, has everything to do with Yahweh." Walter Brueggemann, *Theology of the Old Testament: Testimony, Dispute, Advocacy* (Minneapolis: Fortress Press, 2005), 503.

[16]Terence E. Fretheim, "The Plagues as Ecological Signs," *Journal of Biblical Literature* 110, no. 3 (1991): 393.

[17]For some helpful resources to think about Christian political responsibility and pluralism, see Kristen Deede Johnson, *Theology, Political Theory, and Pluralism: Beyond Tolerance and Difference* (New York: Cambridge University Press, 2007) and Matthew Kaemingk, *Christian Hospitality and Muslim Immigration in an Age of Fear* (Grand Rapids, MI: Eerdmans, 2018).

[18]Makoto Fujimura, *Culture Care: Reconnecting with Beauty for Our Common Life* (Downers Grove, IL: InterVarsity Press, 2017), 106.

[19]Leeman, *Political Church*, 261.

[20]Fujimura, *Culture Care*, 103-4.

5. A Story to Live Into

[1]Stanley Hauerwas, *Approaching the End: Eschatological Reflections on Church, Politics, and Life* (Grand Rapids, MI: Eerdmans, 2013), 93.

[2]Stanley Hauerwas and William H. Willimon, *Resident Aliens: Life in the Christian Colony* (Nashville: Abingdon Press, 2014), 163.

³Brian J. Wright, *Communal Reading in the Time of Jesus: A Window into Early Christian Reading Practices* (Minneapolis: Fortress Press, 2017), 1.

⁴Apol. 39:3, quoted in Wright, *Communal Reading*, 3.

⁵Wright, *Communal Reading*, 3.

⁶Lori Anne Ferrell, *The Bible and the People* (New Haven, CT: Yale University Press, 2008), 27.

⁷Stanley Grenz, *Theology for the Community of God* (Grand Rapids, MI: Eerdmans, 2000), 90.

⁸Karl Barth, *Church Dogmatics* vol 1.1, Sections 1-7: *The Doctrine of the Word of God*, Study Edition 1 (London: T&T Clark, 2010), 74.

⁹James K. A. Smith, *Awaiting the King: Reforming Public Theology* (Grand Rapids, MI: Baker, 2017), 61.

¹⁰Smith, *Awaiting the King*, 61.

¹¹Oliver O'Donovan, "What Kind of Community Is the Church?" *Ecclesiology* 3, no. 2 (January 2007): 71.

¹²Hauerwas and Willimon, *Resident Aliens*, 54.

¹³Matthew Kaemingk, *Christian Hospitality and Muslim Immigration in an Age of Fear* (Grand Rapids, MI: Eerdmans, 2018), 231.

¹⁴John D. Witvliet, *Worship Seeking Understanding* (Grand Rapids, MI: Baker, 2003), 41.

¹⁵Witvliet, *Worship Seeking Understanding*, 43.

¹⁶David P. Gushee and Glen Harold Stassen, *Kingdom Ethics: Following Jesus in Contemporary Context* (Grand Rapids, MI: Eerdmans, 2016), 45.

¹⁷Willie James Jennings, *The Christian Imagination: Theology and the Origins of Race* (New Haven, CT: Yale University Press, 2010).

¹⁸Erwin W. Lutzer, *Hitler's Cross: How the Cross Was Used to Promote the Nazi Agenda* (Chicago: Moody, 2015).

¹⁹William T. Cavanaugh, *Torture and Eucharist: Theology, Politics, and the Body of Christ* (Oxford: Oxford University Press, 1998).

²⁰Hauerwas, *Approaching the End*, 58.

²¹Hauerwas, *Approaching the End*, 68.

²²Hauerwas, *Approaching the End*, 181.

²³Ronald Beiner, *Civil Religion: A Dialogue in the History of Political Philosophy* (Cambridge: Cambridge University Press, 2011), 1-7.

²⁴C. S. Lewis, *An Experiment in Criticism* (Cambridge: Cambridge University Press, 2012), 88.

²⁵This paragraph lightly adapted from Kaitlyn Schiess, "Advent Is Actually Quite Political," *Christ and Pop Culture*, December 11, 2018, https://christandpopculture.com/advent-is-actually-quite-political.

[26]Campbell Robertson, "A Quiet Exodus: Why Black Worshipers Are Leaving White Evangelical Churches," *New York Times*, March 9, 2018, www.nytimes.com/2018/03/09/us/blacks-evangelical-churches.html.

[27]John D. Hannah, *An Uncommon Union: Dallas Theological Seminary and American Evangelicalism* (Grand Rapids, MI: Zondervan, 2009), 180.

[28]Hannah, *An Uncommon Union*, 181.

[29]Mark Noll, "The Peril and Potential of Scripture in Christian Political Witness," in *Christian Political Witness*, ed. George Kalantzis and Gregory W. Lee (Downers Grove, IL: InterVarsity Press, 2014), 40.

[30]Noll, "The Peril and Potential," 42-43.

6. *Ekklēsia*

[1]Dietrich Bonhoeffer, *The Communion of Saints: A Dogmatic Inquiry into the Sociology of the Church* (New York: Harper & Row, 1963), 116.

[2]Brad Harper and Paul Louis Metzger, *Exploring Ecclesiology: An Evangelical and Ecumenical Introduction* (Grand Rapids, MI: Brazos Press, 2009), 29.

[3]Stanley Hauerwas and William H. Willimon, *Resident Aliens: Life in the Christian Colony* (Nashville: Abingdon Press, 2014), 69.

[4]Annie Dillard, *Teaching a Stone to Talk: Expeditions and Encounters* (New York: Harper & Row, 1982), 52-53.

[5]Mark Seifrid, *The Second Letter to the Corinthians*, Pillar New Testament Commentary (Grand Rapids, MI: Eerdmans, 2014), 7.

[6]William T. Cavanaugh, *Migrations of the Holy: God, State, and the Political Meaning of the Church* (Grand Rapids, MI: Eerdmans, 2011), 43.

[7]Donald J. Trump (@realDonaldTrump), Twitter, December 20, 2019.

[8]Stanley Hauerwas, *In Good Company: The Church as Polis* (Notre Dame, IN: University of Notre Dame Press, 1995), 26.

[9]Jonathan Leeman, *Political Church: The Local Assembly as Embassy of Christ's Rule* (Downers Grove, IL: InterVarsity Press, 2016), 368.

[10]Leeman, *Political Church*, 25.

[11]Leeman, *Political Church*, 26.

[12]N. T. Wright, "Paul's Gospel and Caesar's Empire," in *Paul and Politics*, ed. R. A. Horsley (Harrisburg, PA: Trinity Press, 2000), 161-62.

[13]Ellen T. Charry, *By the Renewing of Your Minds: The Pastoral Function of Christian Doctrine* (Oxford: Oxford University Press, 1999), 26.

[14]Charles Chapman Grafton, *The Works of the Rt. Rev. Charles C. Grafton*, ed. Benjamin Talbot Rogers (New York: Longmans, Green & Company, 1914), 284.

[15]Jonathan Edwards, *A Treatise Concerning Religious Affections* (Glasgow, Scotland: Chalmers and Collins, 1825), 75.

[16]Stanley Hauerwas, *Approaching the End: Eschatological Reflections on Church, Politics, and Life* (Grand Rapids, MI: Eerdmans, 2013), ix.

[17]Ephraim Radner, *Hope Among the Fragments: The Broken Church and Its Engagement of Scripture* (Grand Rapids, MI: Brazos, 2004), 50.

[18]John Howard Yoder, *Body Politics: Five Practices of the Christian Community Before the Watching World* (Scottsdale, PA: Herald Press, 1992), 33.

[19]Richard Mouw, "Baptismal Politics," *The Reformed Journal* 28, no. 7 (1978): 2-3.

[20]Mouw, "Baptismal Politics," 2-3.

[21]This section is greatly influenced by R. Alan Streett, *Caesar and the Sacrament: Baptism: A Rite of Resistance* (Eugene, OR: Cascade, 2018), 32.

[22]Streett, *Caesar and the Sacrament*, 126.

[23]Streett, *Caesar and the Sacrament*, 138.

[24]Andrea Bieler and Luise Schottroff, *The Eucharist: Bodies, Bread, and Resurrection* (Minneapolis: Fortress Press, 2007), 74.

[25]Robert E. Webber and Rodney Clapp, *People of the Truth: The Power of the Worshipping Community in the Modern World* (Eugene, OR: Wipf and Stock, 1988), 82.

[26]William T. Cavanaugh, *Torture and Eucharist: Theology, Politics, and the Body of Christ* (Oxford: Oxford University Press, 1998), 205.

[27]James K. A. Smith, *Desiring the Kingdom: Worship, Worldview, and Cultural Formation* (Grand Rapids, MI: Baker Academic, 2009), 162.

[28]Laura Turner, "Internet Church Isn't Really Church," *New York Times*, December 15, 2018, www.nytimes.com/2018/12/15/opinion/sunday/church-live-streaming-religion.html.

[29]Lisa Isherwood and Elizabeth Stuart, *Introducing Body Theology* (London: A&C Black, 1998), 148.

7. The Rhythm of Our Lives

[1]William T. Cavanaugh, *Theopolitical Imagination* (New York: T&T Clark, 2002), 4-5.

[2]Robert Webber, *Ancient-Future Time: Forming Spirituality Through the Christian Year* (Grand Rapids, MI: Baker, 2004), 26.

[3]Scott Bader-Saye, "Figuring Time: Providence and Politics," in *Liturgy, Time, and the Politics of Redemption*, ed. Randi Rashkover and C. C. Pecknold (Grand Rapids, MI: Eerdmans, 2006), 96.

[4]Bader-Saye, "Figuring Time," 220.

[5]Laurence Hull Stookey, *Calendar: Christ's Time for the Church* (Nashville: Abingdon Press, 1996), 23.

⁶Webber, *Ancient-Future Time*, 25.

⁷Martin Connell, *Eternity Today: On the Liturgical Year* (New York: Continuum, 2006), x.

⁸Adapted from Kaitlyn Schiess, "Advent Is Actually Quite Political," *Christ and Pop Culture*, December 11, 2018, https://christandpopculture.com /advent-is-actually-quite-political/.

⁹Fleming Rutledge, *Advent: The Once and Future Coming of Jesus Christ* (Grand Rapids, MI: Eerdmans, 2018), 253.

¹⁰Rutledge, *Advent*, 253.

¹¹Gerald L. Sittser, *Water from a Deep Well: Christian Spirituality from Early Martyrs to Modern Missionaries* (Downers Grove, IL: InterVarsity Press, 2013), 95.

¹²John D. Witvliet, *Worship Seeking Understanding* (Grand Rapids, MI: Baker, 2003), 231.

¹³William W. Reid Jr., "O God of Every Nation," copyright 1958, renewed by The Hymn Society (Carol Stream, IL: Hope Publishing Company, 1986), 958. Cited in Matthew Kaemingk, *Christian Hospitality and Muslim Immigration in an Age of Fear* (Grand Rapids, MI: Eerdmans, 2018), 226-27.

¹⁴Jennifer M. McBride, "Repentance as Political Witness," in *Christian Political Witness*, ed. George Kalantzis and Gregory W. Lee (Downers Grove, IL: InterVarsity Press, 2014), 181.

¹⁵McBride, "Repentance as Political Witness," 182.

¹⁶McBride, "Repentance as Political Witness," 192.

¹⁷McBride, "Repentance as Political Witness," 193.

¹⁸Robert E. Webber and Rodney Clapp, *People of the Truth: The Power of the Worshipping Community in the Modern World* (Eugene, OR: Wipf and Stock, 1988), 73.

¹⁹Tim J. R. Trumper, *Preaching and Politics: Engagement Without Compromise* (Eugene, OR: Wipf and Stock, 2009), 14.

²⁰Nicholas M. Healy, "Practices and the New Ecclesiology: Misplaced Concreteness?" *International Journal of Systematic Theology* 5, no. 3 (2003): 287-308.

²¹Lauren F. Winner, *The Dangers of Christian Practice* (New Haven, CT: Yale University Press, 2018), 3.

²²Nicholas Wolterstorff, *Until Justice and Peace Embrace: The Kuyper Lectures for 1981 Delivered at the Free University of Amsterdam* (Grand Rapids, MI: Eerdmans, 1983), 156.

²³Bernd Wannenwetsch, *Political Worship* (New York: Oxford Press, 2009), 5.

²⁴Wannenwetsch, *Political Worship*, 37.

8. Bent on the Coming Kingdom of God

[1]Kyle David Bennett, *Practices of Love: Spiritual Disciplines for the Life of the World* (Grand Rapids, MI: Brazos, 2017), 7.

[2]Frederick Buechner, *The Longing for Home: Reflection at Midlife* (New York: Harper Collins, 2009), 110.

[3]Lauren F. Winner, *The Dangers of Christian Practice* (New Haven, CT: Yale University Press, 2018), 59.

[4]Barry Jones, *Dwell: Life with God for the World* (Downers Grove, IL: Inter-Varsity Press, 2014), 125.

[5]Dan B. Allender, *Sabbath* (Nashville: Thomas Nelson, 2009), 179.

[6]*The* Book of Pastoral Rule: St. Gregory the Great, ed. George E. Demacopoulos (Yonkers, NY: Saint Vladimirs Seminary Press, 2007), 150.

[7]Aristides, *Apology*, in *The Early Christians in their Own Words*, ed. Eberhard Arnold (Walden, NY: Plough, 1970), 109-11.

[8]Douglas Kaine McKlevey, "A Liturgy for Feasting with Friends," Rabbit Room, November 24, 2016, https://rabbitroom.com/2016/11/a-liturgy-for-feasting -with-friends/.

[9]Henri Nouwen, *Reaching Out: The Three Movements of the Spiritual Life* (New York: Image Books, 1975), 66.

[10]Mandate 8:8-10, *The Apostolic Fathers*, ed. Michael W. Holmes, 2nd ed. (Grand Rapids, MI: Baker, 1992), 397.

[11]Christine D. Pohl, *Making Room: Recovering Hospitality as a Christian Tradition* (Grand Rapids, MI: Eerdmans, 1999), 5.

[12]Quoted in Robert Coles, *Dorothy Day: A Radical Devotion* (Lebanon, IN: Da Capo Press, 1989), 40.

[13]Nouwen, *Reaching Out*, 65-66.

[14]Joshua W. Jipp, *Saved by Faith and Hospitality* (Grand Rapids, MI: Eerdmans, 2017), 18.

[15]Jipp, *Saved by Faith and Hospitality*, 157-58.

[16]Jipp, Saved *by Faith and Hospitality*, 158.

[17]Chrysostom, Homily 21 on Romans, *Nicene and Post-Nicene Fathers* 1, vol. 11, 505.

[18]C. S. Lewis, *Reflections on the Psalms* (Boston: Houghton Mifflin Harcourt, 1958), 26-27.

9. A Confessing City

[1]The degree to which Augustine's theology and political theory allow for Christian political engagement is a source of much academic discussion. However, the tension between his pessimism and activism is pretty universally

acknowledged. For an overview of the different ways scholars have read *City of God*, see Gregory Lee and Anthony Dupont, "Augustine's Two Cities Revisited: Contemporary Approaches to Dei civitate Dei," *History of Philosophy and Social Thought* 61 (2016), 101-4.

[2]For one example: Augustine, *Ep. 134, Political Writings*, eds. E. M. Atkins and R. J. Dodero (New York: Cambridge University Press, 2007), 64.

[3]Eric Gregory, *Politics and the Order of Love: An Augustinian Ethic of Democratic Citizenship* (Chicago: University of Chicago Press, 2008), 52. Also see Augustine, *De civitate Dei*, 5.19.

[4]Augustine, *Ep. 155, Political Writings,* 89.

[5]Robert Dodaro, "Augustine on the Statesman and the Two Cities," in *A Companion to Augustine*, ed. Mark Vessey (Hoboken, NJ: Wiley, 2015), 388.

[6]Gregory, *Politics and the Order of Love*, 361.

[7]Augustine, *De civitate Dei*, 4.3; *Confessiones*, 10.39-66.

[8]Augustine, *De civitate Dei*, 1.15.

[9]Robert Dodaro, *Christ and the Just Society in the Thought of Augustine* (New York: Cambridge University Press, 2004), 27.

[10]Gregory Lee, "Using the Earthly City: Ecclesiology, Political Activity, and Religious Coercion in Augustine," *Augustinian Studies* 47, no. 1 (2016): 54.

[11]Charles Mayo Collier, "A Nonviolent Augustinianism?: History and Politics in the Theologies of St. Augustine and John Howard Yoder" (PhD diss., Duke University, 2008), 97.

[12]Charles T. Mathewes, *The Republic of Grace: Augustinian Thoughts for Dark Times* (Grand Rapids, MI: Eerdmans, 2010), 234.

[13]Richard Luman, "Journeys and Gardens: Narrative Patterns in the Confessiones of St. Augustine," in *Collectanea Augustiniana*, ed. Joseph Schnaubelt and Frederick van Fleteren (New York: Lang, 1990), 142.

[14]Mathewes, *Republic of Grace*, 80.

[15]Mathewes, *Republic of Grace*, 80.

[16]Charles T. Mathewes, "Book One: The Presumptuousness of Autobiography and the Paradoxes of Beginning," in *A Reader's Companion to Augustine's Confessions*, ed. Kim Paffenroth and Robert P. Kennedy (Louisville, KY: Westminster John Knox, 2003), 7.

[17]R. A. Markus, *Saeculum: History and Society in the Theology of St. Augustine* (New York: Cambridge, 1988), 16.

[18]Gregory Lee, "Republics and Their Loves: Rereading *City of God* 19," *Modern Theology* 27, no. 4 (2011): 553.

[19]Lee, "Republics and Their Loves," 553.

20Theodor E. Mommsen, "Christian Idea of Progress," in *The City of God: A Collection of Critical Essays*, ed. Dorothy F. Donnelly (New York: Peter Lang, 1995), 368.

21Even when ascribing judgement to Rome in book one, Augustine sticks primarily to descriptions of how God can work, something scriptural history tells us: he "constantly uses war to correct and chasten the corrupt morals of mankind," something he knows from Scripture, not from his own judgement on Rome (*De civitate Dei*, 1.1).

22Augustine, *De civitate Dei*, 1.8.

23See Evan Berryhill, "Why 2016 May Be the Most Important Election of Our Lifetime," *The Hill*, July 20, 2016, https://thehill.com/blogs/congress-blog/presidential-campaign/288551-why-2016-may-actually-be-the-most-important, and Franklin Graham, "The Most Important Election of Our Lifetime," *Decision*, Sept 20, 2016, https://decisionmagazine.com/most-important-election-lifetime/.

24Andrew R. Murphy, "Augustine and the Rhetoric of Roman Decline," in *Augustine and History*, ed. Christopher T. Daly, John Doody, and Kim Paffenroth (New York: Lexington Books, 2008), 68-69.

25James K. A. Smith, *Awaiting the King: Reforming Public Theology* (Grand Rapids, MI: Baker, 2017), 217.

26Rowan Williams, "Politics and the Soul: A Reading of the City of God," *Milltown Studies* 19/20 (1987): 65.

27Augustine, *De civitate Dei*, 5.26.

28Christopher Dawson, "The City of God," in *A Monument to Saint Augustine*, ed. Martin Cyril Darcy (London: Sheed and Ward, 1945), 44-45.

29For example, he included it among the "divine institutions" in *On Christian Doctrine*, 2.38-44.

30Oliver O'Donovan, *Desire of the Nations: Rediscovering the Roots of Political Theology* (Cambridge: Cambridge University Press, 1999), 2.

31James Wetzel, *Augustine's City of God: A Critical Guide* (New York: Cambridge University Press, 2012), 51.

32Peter Dennis Bathory, *Political Theory as Public Confession: The Social and Political Thought of St. Augustine of Hippo* (Piscataway, NJ: Transaction Books, 1981), 150.

33Jean Bethke Elshtain, *Augustine and the Limits of Politics* (Notre Dame, IN: Notre Dame University Press, 1995), 15.

34Peter Brown, *Augustine of Hippo: A Biography* (Berkeley: University of California Press, 1967), 308.

[35]Gregory, *Politics and the Order of Love*, 52.

[36]John von Heyking, *Augustine and Politics as Longing in the World* (Columbia: University of Missouri Press, 2001), 261.

[37]Lee, "Republics and their Loves," 574.

10. Creation Redeemed

[1]Bruce David Forbes, "How Popular Are the Left Behind Books . . . and Why?" in *Rapture, Revelation, and The End Times: Exploring the Left Behind Series* (New York: Palgrave MacMillan, 2004), 8-9.

[2]Dietrich Bonhoeffer, *Creation and Fall: A Theological Exposition of Genesis 1-3* (Minneapolis: Fortress Press, 1997), 21.

[3]N. T. Wright, *Surprised by Hope: Rethinking Heaven, the Resurrection, and the Mission of the Church* (New York: Harper One, 2008), 27.

[4]Glenn R. Kreider, "The Flood Is as Bad as It Gets: Never Again Will God Destroy the Earth," *Bibliotheca Sacra* 171, no. 684 (2014): 425-27.

[5]For some analysis on Aronofsky and religious subject matter, see Alissa Wilkinson, "Mother! Will Infuriate Many Viewers. In 2014, Darren Aronofsky's Film Noah Did the Same," *Vox*, September 16, 2017, www.vox.com/culture/2017/9/16/16316960/mother-noah-movie-of-week-aronofsky-f-cinemascore.

[6]Andy Crouch, *Culture Making: Recovering Our Creative Calling* (Downers Grove, IL: InterVarsity Press, 2008), 103.

[7]*The Man Who Planted Trees*, directed by Frédéric Back (Ottawa: CBC, 1987).

[8]Richard J. Mouw, *When the Kings Come Marching In: Isaiah and the New Jerusalem* (Grand Rapids, MI: Eerdmans, 2002), 20.

[9]Wright, *Surprised by Hope*, 100.

[10]Wright, *Surprised by Hope*, 133.

[11]Frank Jehle, *Ever Against the Stream: The Politics of Karl Barth, 1906-1968* (Eugene, OR: Wipf and Stock, 2012), 32-33.

[12]Marianne Meye Thompson, "Reading What Is Written in the Book of Life: Theological Interpretation of the Book of Revelation Today," in *Revelation and the Politics of Apocalyptic Interpretation*, ed. Richard B. Hays and Stefan Alkier (Waco, TX: Baylor University Press, 2012), 166.

[13]John J. Collins, "Apocalyptic Literature," in *Early Judaism and Its Modern Interpreters*, ed. R. A. Kraft and G. W. E. Nickelsburg (Philadelphia and Atlanta: Fortress and Scholars Press, 1989), 345.

[14]Flannery O'Connor, *Mystery and Manners: Occasional Prose* (London: Macmillan, 1969), 34.

[15]David Dark, *Everyday Apocalypse: The Sacred Revealed in Radiohead, the Simpsons, and Other Pop Culture Icons* (Grand Rapids, MI: Brazos, 2002), 19.

[16]Michael J. Gorman, *Reading Revelation Responsibly: Uncivil Worship and Witness* (Eugene, OR: Cascade Books, 2011), 46.

[17]Gorman, *Reading Revelation Responsibly*, 53.

[18]Wayne A. Meeks, *The Moral World of the First Christians* (Philadelphia: Westminster, 1986), 145.

[19]Oliver O'Donovan, *Desire of the Nations: Rediscovering the Roots of Political Theology* (Cambridge: Cambridge University Press, 1999), 155.

[20]Richard B. Hays, *The Moral Vision of the New Testament: A Contemporary Introduction to New Testament Ethics* (New York: Harper Collins, 1996), 177.

[21]Richard Bauckham, *The Theology of the Book of Revelation* (Cambridge: Cambridge University Press, 1993), 160.

[22]Bauckham, *The Theology of the Book of Revelation*, 160.

[23]N. T. Wright, "Revelation and Christian Hope," in *Revelation and the Politics of Apocalyptic Interpretation*, eds. Richard B. Hays and Stefan Alkier (Waco, TX: Baylor University Press, 2015), 107.

[24]James K. A. Smith, *Awaiting the King: Reforming Public Theology* (Grand Rapids, MI: Baker, 2017), 89.

[25]Robert E. Webber and Rodney Clapp, *People of the Truth: The Power of the Worshipping Community in the Modern World* (Eugene, OR: Wipf and Stock, 1988), 57.

Epilogue: *Shalom*

[1]Walter Brueggemann, *Like Fire in the Bones: Listening for the Prophetic Word in Jeremiah* (Minneapolis: Fortress Press, 2006), 27.